SRA Open Court Reading
Language Arts Handbook

Grade 3

Mc
Graw
Hill
Education

MHEonline.com

Send all inquiries to:
McGraw-Hill Education
8787 Orion Place
Columbus, OH 43240

ISBN: 978-0-07-668590-5
MHID: 0-07-668590-X

Printed in the United States of America.

3 4 5 6 7 8 9 LWI 25 24 23 22

Table of Contents

SECTION 1 ## The Writing Process 18

SECTION 2 Forms of Writing 56

SECTION 3

Writing Strategies 232

SECTION 5 Grammar, Usage, and Mechanics 338

You Are a Writer! . . . .

Everyone is a writer. You are a writer. Your friend sitting next to you is. Look around you. Everyone you see is a writer.

What Do You Write?

Have you ever made a list of school supplies you needed? Have you ever written a note to your parents? Have you ever written about how to make your favorite food? Maybe you have written a make-believe story. These are a few examples of the kinds of writing you do. Some are long. Some are short. You have probably done many of them already.

When Can You Write?

Anytime! Some people like to write in a journal or a diary before they go to sleep. Others write down words or jokes they might want to use later. Every day, there are many chances to write.

Where Can You Write?

Anywhere! You probably write sitting at a table or desk most of the time, but you can get ideas anywhere. Whether you are outdoors or in your bed, take a second to jot down your ideas.

Why Write?

Everybody has thoughts that are worth sharing. Writing is a way to share your thoughts, ideas, and feelings with others.

How Do You Write?

That question can't be answered in a couple of sentences. That's why there is a lot of help with writing in this book. You will also find information on spelling, punctuation, studying, using the computer, and much more.

The Traits of Good Writing

Good writers are not born good writers. They learn to be good writers. How? They do it by studying and practicing the traits of good writing. The traits of good writing are certain qualities that make reading it enjoyable. These traits are described below and on the following pages.

Ideas

Your ideas should be clear, original, and supported by details. Ideas are the heart of your writing. Good ideas are supported by colorful details that make writing interesting to a reader. Your writing should have a main idea that sends a clear message to the reader. Use accurate details to support your idea.

EXAMPLE Read this paragraph from "A New Life for Mei" by Judy Kentor Schmauss.

> Mei and Hong left China in 1867 to start a new life. Hong's uncle had come to America in 1849, looking for gold. Although he was very poor, he sent letters home detailing his travels in America. He was not one of the lucky few to strike it rich, but he enjoyed his adventures in the new land. Due to his letters, Hong and Mei decided to try their own luck in San Francisco.

When you read the paragraph, did you think, "I want to know more about this story. I want to find out what happens to Mei and Hong in San Francisco"? The author gave enough details to make the reader curious about the characters Mei and Hong.

Organization

Your writing should have:

▶ a beginning that interests the reader right away
▶ a sequence that makes sense
▶ a good ending

A reader who is not interested in your beginning probably will not keep reading for very long. That is why your first few sentences or paragraphs should convince the reader that he or she should read on to the end.

The sequence of events or information should make sense to the reader. If you tell about something that happened in the past, make sure the reader can easily tell that it happened in the past.

Your ending should leave the reader thinking, "That was really good. I will tell my friends to read this."

EXAMPLE   Read the end of "A New Life for Mei."

Having heard that Mei's husband was back, Mr. Fischer came in and shook Hong's hand. Hong felt proud of Mei and proud of the community that had come together. Starting a new life in America had turned out to be a good idea after all.

The beginning of the story makes you want to find out if Mei and Hong like their new home in San Francisco, and the ending gives you the answer.

Voice

Your writing should sound as though you are:

▶ aware of your audience
▶ involved in the topic

Each writer has his or her own voice. Your voice is what makes your writing different from anyone else's. You should always keep in mind who your audience is so you can try to connect to them. You should care about your topic so you can make your audience care. When you care about your topic and want to share it with your readers, your enthusiasm comes through.

EXAMPLE

Mei loved what she was doing. She poured her heart into making everything run smoothly. She was always looking for new dishes to prepare. As a result, the restaurant became even more popular.

In this paragraph from "A New Life for Mei," the author uses specific words and phrases to show that Mei is happy to be working in the restaurant. The author's voice helps the reader sense Mei's enjoyment with her job.

Vocabulary Strategies

The words you choose should:

▶ be precise
▶ be original
▶ help create a picture in the reader's mind

You should not repeat words too much. You should use words that are precise. For example, instead of using the word *flower*, you might use the word *rose*, which is more precise. You should use vocabulary words that help the reader see what you are describing.

EXAMPLE

Mei was apprehensive about being alone in the city. The people of Chinatown worked together to support each other, but there were few jobs, and Mei spoke less English than Hong. She did not know how she would manage.

Everyone has felt overwhelmed at one time or another. Sometimes it is scary to move to a new place and to have new experiences. We can understand Mei's anxious feelings in the author's choice of the words *apprehensive, alone,* and *manage.* Can you remember a time when something was new to you? Maybe the first day at a new school? Were you nervous or apprehensive? How did you manage?

Try It!

Replace words in the following sentence to create a better image.
Joe watched the snow falling.

Sentence Fluency

Your sentences should:

▶ be pleasing
▶ flow
▶ have rhythm

Always read your sentences aloud. The sentences you write should flow like the sentences you use when you speak. If you listen to your sentences and those of others, you will get an idea of the styles of sentences that you like to hear and read. Writing that has only short sentences does not flow. Writing that has only long sentences can be difficult to follow. There should be a good mix of long and short sentences in your writing.

EXAMPLE **Read the sentences from "A New Life for Mei" aloud. Notice how well they fit together. Listen to how they flow.**

Mei worked hard for the next two days. The meal she served Mr. Fischer and his business partners was quickly devoured. As the evening ended, it was clear that everything went off without a hitch. Mr. Fischer was so impressed that he came back every night for a week. Each time, he brought more and more guests. Mei knew she needed help.

Notice that there are some short sentences and some long ones. Also, notice that not every sentence begins with a subject.

Conventions

You should always check your:

▶ spelling
▶ punctuation
▶ capitalization
▶ usage

Your writing will be easier to read if it is free of mistakes. Readers stumble over mistakes, trying to fix them in their minds before going on. That interrupts the flow of reading. Sometimes you don't know where your mistakes are. A teacher, parent, or friend can help you find the mistakes, and they can help you figure out how to fix them.

Presentation

How writing looks on a page is important. This is called **presentation**. Your written work should be neatly typed or handwritten. Writing and illustrations on a page should be pleasing to the reader.

Reading Your Writing

The traits of good writing are ideas, organization, voice, word choice, sentence fluency, conventions, and presentation. Think about the traits of good writing as you write fiction, nonfiction, and poetry. By using these traits, you will make your writing more enjoyable for your readers.

The Writing Process

There are five parts to the writing process: prewriting, drafting, revising, editing/proofreading, and publishing. You can use them to become a better writer.

The Writing Process

You write some things quickly, such as a note to remember something. Other things, such as stories and reports, take more time and thought. To help you with all kinds of writing, use the **writing process**. It can help you organize your writing and make it the best it can be.

STEP 1 Prewriting

This is where it all begins. This can take a while because there is a lot of thinking and writing to do. You can use your prewriting time to:

- think about what you want to say
- write down your ideas
- collect information
- think about who will read your writing
- decide if you are writing to entertain, to inform, to persuade, or to explain
- organize your ideas on paper

STEP 2 Drafting

This is the time to get some of your ideas down on paper. You should write quickly while your best thoughts are in your mind. You should not worry too much about spelling, punctuation, or handwriting.

STEP 3 Revising

During revising, you have a chance to change your writing to make it better. You can read it out loud to hear how it sounds. You can change and rearrange words, sentences, and paragraphs to make your ideas clearer. You can ask a friend to read it and tell you what is good and what could be better. You can talk to your teacher about how to make your writing better.

STEP 4 Editing/Proofreading

This is when you need to look at spelling and usage. If words are misspelled, or if you've used the wrong words, your readers may not be able to figure out what you are saying. You can make a list of problems that you want to look for in your writing and then read your writing over and over, checking one thing at a time.

STEP 5 Publishing

This is your chance to make your writing look good. Using your best handwriting or a computer, you can make a clean copy of your writing. You can add pictures, charts, or diagrams. You can bind it in a book, submit it to a magazine, or mail it if it is a letter.

Reading Your Writing

The writing process will help you organize, improve, and correct your writing. Put your writing aside between each step. This helps you take a fresh look at your writing.

STEP 1 Prewriting

Follow the writing process for any kind of writing. The writing process includes **prewriting, drafting, revising, editing/proofreading,** and **publishing.** You may not always use all of these steps, but when you do, they can help you write better. Mia uses them. Follow along as Mia shows how she used the writing process for the writing tasks. Mia started with the first step, which is **prewriting.**

Understanding the Task, Purpose, and Audience

Mia's teacher asked her students to each write a paragraph describing something. Mia had to think about and answer three questions before she got started.

1. **Task** What kind of writing are you going to do?
2. **Purpose** Will you write to entertain, to give information, to explain, or to persuade?
3. **Audience** Who will be reading your writing?

Task

This was easy for Mia. Her teacher wanted her to write a description.

Purpose

Mia thought about why she would write a description. She decided that her purpose was to explain.

Audience

Mia decided that her audience would be her new pen pal, who lives in Sierra Leone. Mia would have to think of something she knew about that he might find interesting.

Try It!

Imagine that your teacher told you to write a story about a dog. What would your task be? Who would be your audience? What would be your purpose?

Getting and Narrowing Ideas

Mia needed to decide exactly what she would describe. She wanted to choose something that her pen pal would find interesting and that she knew well. She thought about her house, the family car, her pet dog, and her little brother. Then she asked her friends for ideas. She made a list.

	my house
	my family's car
	my pet dog
	my little brother
	my face
	Guy's red bicycle
	Sears Tower
	cornstalks on Grandpa's farm

Try It!

Imagine describing something to Mia's pen pal in Sierra Leone. What ideas do you and your friends have about the kinds of things you might describe?

Choosing a Topic

Now that Mia had some ideas, she had to choose one idea to write about. How did she do that? She asked herself:

▶ What would my pen pal want to read about?
▶ I want to explain something, so which thing on my list do I know the most about?
▶ Which thing on my list can I describe the best?

Mia looked over her list carefully. She thought that her pen pal had probably seen bicycles, cars, and cornstalks, so those things wouldn't be anything new to him. The Sears Tower is a tall, brown building, so Mia thought that wouldn't be very interesting to describe. Finally, Mia decided that because her pen pal had never seen her, she would describe her own face.

Try It!

Ask yourself the same questions Mia asked herself. What idea would you choose from your earlier list?

FUN fact

Sierra Leone is a country on Africa's western coast. Monkeys, chimpanzees, tigers, porcupines, antelope, and crocodiles live there.

Organizing Ideas

This part worried Mia the most. She was very unorganized. Her desk was always a mess. She often lost her homework. She forgot where she put her shoes almost every day.

Mia needed help organizing her ideas. Luckily, her teacher said, "Remember, you can use graphic organizers to help you organize your ideas." Mia let out a huge sigh. Now she had somewhere to begin.

A **graphic organizer** is a diagram that helps a writer put ideas in an order that makes sense. Mia decided to try a web.

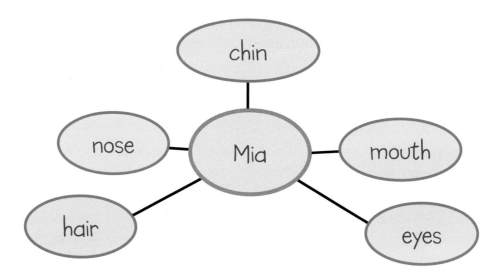

Mia thought this was a good start, but she needed more details for a good description. She also needed to put the details in order. Mia tried to think of other organizers.

TREE Diagram

The next graphic organizer Mia remembered was the TREE graphic organizer. She used the TREE diagram to remember the different sections of the graphic organizer. They looked like this:

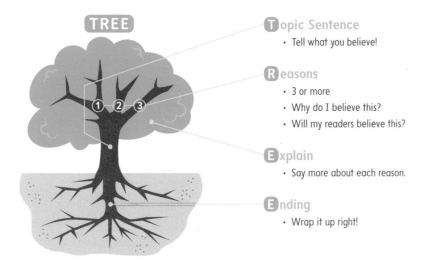

T	Topic Sentence
R	Reasons—3 or more
E	Explanations
E	Ending

Since the TREE graphic organizer helps to organize ideas for informative writing and opinion writing, Mia knew that a TREE graphic organizer would not work for her descriptive writing.

Chain of Events

Then Mia thought of another graphic organizer. It shows events in the order they happen.

Chain of Events

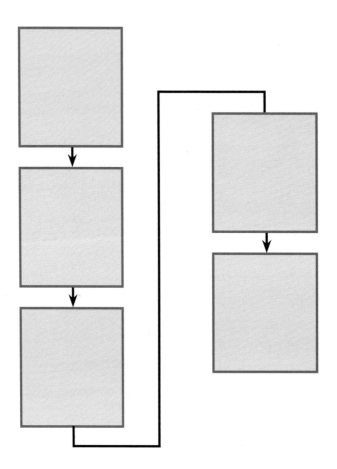

Mia was stumped. What other organizer could she use? She knew she needed to organize the details in her description. Mia looked at her face closely in a mirror. "That's it!" she exclaimed. Mia realized that she had looked at her face from top to bottom. She decided to organize her description the same way.

Spatial Order

Mia came up with this graphic organizer herself. Notice that she put what she was describing, her face, at the top. Then she put details about her face in order from top to bottom in the other boxes.

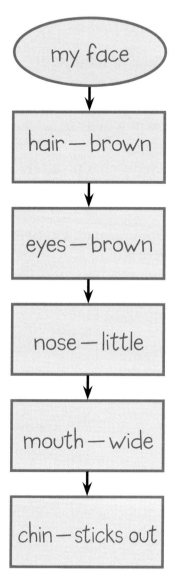

This graphic organizer helped Mia put her ideas in an order that would be easy for her reader to follow. Mia found out that prewriting can take a long time but that it will be very helpful when she writes her draft.

STEP 2 Drafting

The next step in the writing process is **drafting**. In this step, Mia used the information in her graphic organizer to write a draft. She tried to keep her audience in mind as she wrote.

Mia knew that she had to write her thoughts down quickly. Here are some helpful hints she used to do that.

▶ Don't worry about spelling, punctuation, or handwriting.
▶ Write on every other line. This will give you room to add things later.
▶ Use abbreviations or write the sounds you hear in a word that you can't spell.
▶ Cross out or circle words that you plan to change later.
▶ Leave blanks when you can't think of a word.

Mia looked at the information in her graphic organizer. She wasn't sure if she should write a single paragraph or separate paragraphs for each of the boxes in her organizer. She thought that one paragraph would be enough. First, she wrote a topic sentence that told the main idea.

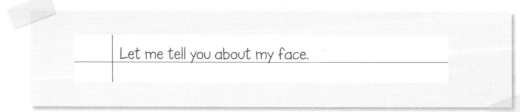

Let me tell you about my face.

Beginning to Write

Then, Mia wrote a separate sentence for each detail in her graphic organizer.

Let me tell you about my face.

My hair is brown. It is strate.

My eyes are brown My friend has

blue eyes. my chin is p_____y.

My nose is kind of small. My

mouth is kind of big. My feet

are huge.

Reading Your Writing

During drafting it is important to get your ideas on paper quickly. That way, you won't forget any of them.

STEP 3 Revising

When you are done with your draft, it is a good idea to put it aside for a while. You might get some new ideas when you aren't thinking so hard about your writing. You make your writing better during **revising**. If you have written your draft on a computer, you may want to save each new version in a separate file.

Mia knew that revising also takes a while. She would need to read her writing several times, looking for ways to improve it. She would also let her classmates read her writing. They might spot ways to improve her description that she may have missed. Mia knew that these questions based on the traits of writing would also help.

Ideas
▶ Is the main idea clear?
▶ Do I stay on the topic?

Organization
▶ Do I follow the order I decided on in prewriting?

Vocabulary Strategies
▶ Do I repeat some words too often?
▶ Do I use the best words to describe my face?

Sentence Fluency
▶ Do my sentences read smoothly?
▶ Do I use sentences that are too short or too long?

Voice
▶ Do I show my audience my face with words?

Staying on Topic

Mia doesn't want her audience to become confused, so she read her description once to make sure that all of her sentences were about the topic she chose. Because Mia is describing her face, all of her sentences should be about some part of her face. Mia read her description to make sure that all of the sentences were about the main idea. Mia realized that she had a sentence about her feet. Why did she put that in there? She crossed it out. She also thought of a couple of details she wanted to add.

Let me tell you about my face.

My hair is brown. It is strate.

My eyes are brown My friend has

blue eyes. my chin is p_____y.

It has frekiles all over it.
My nose is kind of small. My

but my lips are skinny.
mouth is kind of big. My feet

are huge

Try It!

Mia has another sentence in her description that doesn't belong. Which one is it?

Coherence

Next, Mia made sure her description was in an order that made sense. During prewriting, she had decided to describe her face from top to bottom. Mia had thought that this way of describing her face would help her pen pal picture her.

Mia read her description out loud and thought of two things. First, she had kept the order of her description of her face from top to bottom except for one sentence. The sentence about her chin should go last. Mia marked the sentence to remember to move it later.

Second, Mia noticed that some of her sentences were choppy. She thought that adding words to these sentences would make them smoother. She added the phrases *at the top of my head, below that, next,* and *at the bottom.*

Linking Words

Linking words such as the words Mia added to her paragraph helps sentences to flow smoothly. These words connect or link ideas together. Examples of linking words include the following:

additionally	before	soon
after	finally	throughout
again	first	when
also	later	at the top
another	meanwhile	on the other hand
behind	next	as a result

Try It!

Think of three sentences that you could put together using the words *first, then,* and *finally.*

Let me tell you about my face. *At the top of my head is*

My hair is red brown and strate. *Below that*

Next is
My eyes are brown ~~My friend has~~

~~blue eyes.~~ my chin is p_____y.

small   *It has frekiles all over it*
My nose. ~~is kind of small.~~ My

but my lips are skinny
mouth is kind of big. ~~My feet~~

At the bottom is my chin.
~~are huge.~~

Adding Variety

Mia realized that writing requires a lot of work to keep readers interested. To keep readers interested, you must have some variety. If you don't have variety, your readers will get bored. If you have too much variety, your readers will not enjoy your writing. You can add variety to your writing by:

- using specific words to create a clear picture
- varying sentence length—use some short and some long sentences
- taking out extra words
- varying the beginnings of sentences
- beginning a paragraph with a question

Because her pen pal had never seen her, Mia had to *show* him what she looks like with her words, not just tell him. She would need to choose words that would create a clear and vivid picture for him. In her draft, Mia had said that she had brown hair. Mia thought about this again: "Well, there are many different colors of brown hair. There are dark brown, light brown, and red-brown." Mia decided that she would need to be more specific if she wanted her pen pal to really be able to "see" her hair.

Try It!

Think about your hair color. What specific words could you use to describe the color of your hair?

Conferencing

Your classmates can be a big help during the revising process. They can give you one last, fresh look at your writing. Having a **conference** with one or more classmates is a way to find out what is good in your writing and what can be better.

There are two roles in a conference: writers and listeners. During a conference, the writer asks other students to listen to and comment on his or her writing.

Here are some things that a writer and listeners do in a conference.

During a conference, the writer	The writer needs to remember that
▷ reads his or her work out loud.	▷ listeners are trying to help.
▷ records others' comments.	▷ most writing can be improved.
▷ decides which comments to use.	▷ it is good to get feedback from others.
▷ marks his or her paper for revisions.	▷ he or she will make the final decisions.

During a conference, listeners	The listeners need to remember
▷ point out things they liked.	▷ to respect the writer's hard work.
▷ point out places they had trouble understanding.	▷ that everybody wants to hear good things about his or her writing.
	▷ to listen carefully and be polite.

Everyone must remember to be helpful, not hurtful, during conferences. Here are some rules that will help conferences go smoothly.

Rules for Good Conferences

1. Listen quietly when others are speaking.
2. Think carefully before you say anything about another person's work.
3. Be specific.
4. Tell something you like before you tell what can be improved.
5. Discuss quietly so you do not disturb others who are working nearby.

Try It!

Ask a couple of friends to listen to something that you have written. Ask them to tell one thing they liked and one thing they think could be better.

FUN fact

A conference is a meeting between two or more people to discuss something. The word conference has been in use for about 500 years!

EXAMPLE Mia asked Miguel and Jenny to help her with her writing. She read to them. Here are their comments.

Miguel: I like the descriptive words you used. I can definitely picture your face.

Jenny: You included all of the features on your face.

Miguel: You could change your first sentence to a question to get people's attention.

Jenny: Maybe you could change some of your sentences so they don't all start with the word "My."

After the Conference

Mia wrote the comments from Miguel and Jenny. Then she thanked them for their help. Next she will take their comments and decide what she is going to change. She will make changes to improve her writing.

Reading Your Writing

Writing takes a lot of time and effort. Sometimes your writing is not clear to your audience. Revising, staying on topic, adding variety, and conferencing are all ways that you can make your writing better. It is also a good idea to have others listen to and comment on your writing.

STEP 4 Editing/Proofreading

The next step is **editing/proofreading**, where you will look at the conventions of writing. The conventions of writing are spelling, grammar, usage, and mechanics. You will correct misspelled words. You will look for punctuation errors. You will make sure that you have used capital letters where they belong. You will make sure that your sentences are complete and that they read smoothly.

Using Proofreading Marks

Mia planned to use special marks on her paper to show where she needed to make corrections. These are called **proofreading marks**. Mia liked using them because they saved her time and they showed her what needed to be rewritten. Here are the proofreading marks that Mia knows.

¶ Indent the paragraph.

∧ Add something.

⸌ Take out something.

/ Make a small letter.

≡ Make a capital letter.

sp
◯ Check spelling.

⊙ Add a period.

Try It!

Look at Mia's revised description on page 35. What proofreading marks do you think she will need to use?

Using an Editing/Proofreading Checklist

Mia's teacher helped her make an editing/proofreading checklist. That way she wouldn't forget to check for spelling errors, sentence fragments, or missing punctuation.

▶ Each sentence begins with a capital letter.
▶ Each sentence ends with the correct punctuation.
▶ Commas are used in compound sentences.
▶ Each sentence is complete.
▶ Each word is spelled correctly.
▶ The paragraph is indented.

Here is Mia's edited paragraph.

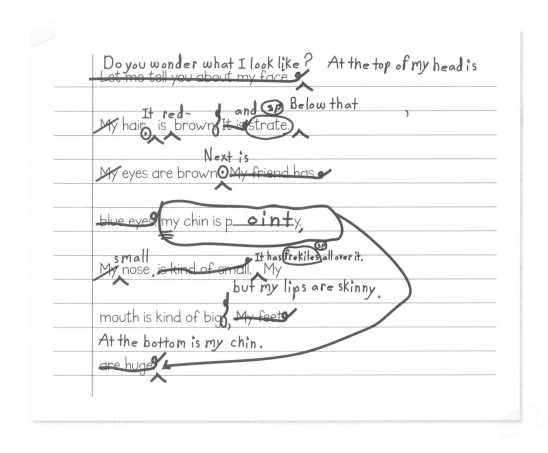

Good Presentation

Because Mia's teacher wants her to hand in her letter to her pen pal, she will prepare a neat copy that will be easy to read. She will use her best handwriting. Then she will check this copy against her edited copy to make sure she has put in all of the changes she wanted to make.

> Do you wonder what I look like? At the top of my head is my hair. It is red-brown and straight. Below that, my eyes are brown. Next is my small nose. It has freckles all over it. My mouth is kind of big, but my lips are skinny. At the bottom is my chin. My chin is pointy.

Editing/Proofreading on a Computer

If you have written your paper on a computer, you may want to use the spelling and grammar tools to edit/proofread it. You should still read your printed copy for errors.

Here are some tips.

To insert punctuation or words	Move the cursor to the correct place and type in the change.
To check spelling	Click on the spell-check button.
To indent paragraphs	Place the cursor in front of the first word in the paragraph, then press the tab key.
To move text	Select the text to be moved, then click the cut button. Move the cursor to where you want the text, then click on the paste button.

WARNING: Spell-checkers will not catch all spelling mistakes. You may use the wrong word but spell it correctly. Spell-checkers won't catch this type of mistake.

EXAMPLE A spell-checker missed the two mistakes in the following sentence. Do you know why?

should be to ▶ James went too the story. ◀ should be store

STEP 5 Publishing

The last step in the writing process is **publishing**. At this stage, you are ready to share your writing with others. If you haven't already, you need to make a clean copy in your best handwriting or on the computer. The form in which you choose to publish your writing depends on what kind of writing it is and who your audience is. You should choose the best way to share what you have done for the audience that you have chosen.

Ways to Publish

If your writing is a story, you could make it a book and put it in the reading center.

How to Make a Book	
1. Fold some 8 ½ by 11-inch paper in half.	**4.** Draw pictures or add charts, tables, or diagrams.
2. Staple it in the middle.	**5.** Put a construction paper cover on it.
3. Write your story on the pages.	**6.** Write the title and your name on the cover.

If it is a letter, you should mail it.

If it is a play or a story, you could act it out.

If it is a description, you could illustrate it and put it on a bulletin board. That is what Mia has decided for now. Later, she will include it in a letter to her pen pal. Then she will mail it to him.

To Publish or Not to Publish

You may not publish every piece of writing you create. To decide if you want to publish something, ask yourself,

▶ Is this my best piece?
▶ Should I publish this type of writing?
▶ Who will read my writing?
▶ Have I revised it to make it better?
▶ Have I proofread it carefully?

You will also want to think about what more you can do with your piece of writing. Perhaps you can add something. What you choose to add will depend again on what kind of writing it is, the way you plan to publish, and your audience. Here are some things you might add.

▶ Photographs can be used in a description, a story about yourself, or a biography. Remember to write captions.
▶ A chart or a graph can be used in an article.
▶ A diagram can be used if you have explained how to make something or how something works.
▶ Drawings or diagrams can be used to illustrate a point or add interest to your writing.

Try It!

Think about a piece of writing you have done recently. To publish this piece, what could you add to it?

Using Charts, Tables and Diagrams

You may choose to add charts, tables, and diagrams to your writing. Charts and tables can show a lot of information in a small amount of space. Diagrams can clearly illustrate something you are explaining. You might want to use one of these in your writing if it will help your reader understand what you are saying.

Using a Chart or Table

If you have similar information about several items in your writing, you can put it in an easy-to-read chart or table.

EXAMPLE

Favorite Cafeteria Lunch

	Roasted Chicken	Turkey Burger	Taco
First Grade	X		
Second Grade			X
Third Grade		X	
Fourth Grade			X
Fifth Grade		X	

Try It!

What do you know by studying the table above?
You can create charts and tables by drawing them, or you can make them on a computer.

Using a Diagram

A diagram can be helpful if you are explaining something. For example, if you are describing the parts of a bicycle, you could put a diagram of a bike in your paper and label it. This would make what you are saying clearer. It can also add information to what you have written. It would be boring to tell the location of all the bike parts. With a diagram, that information is easy to see.

EXAMPLE

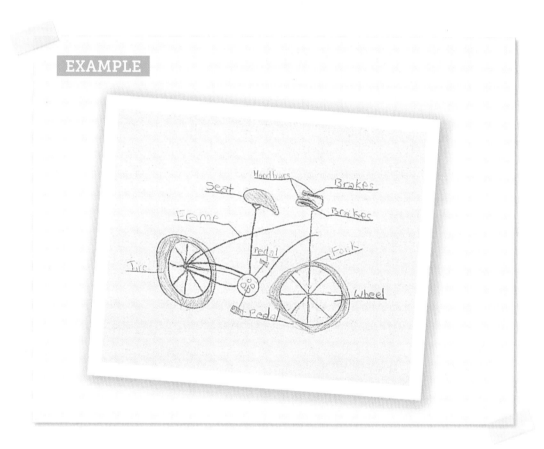

Try It!

Imagine that you are describing how to build a kite. Would you describe it with a chart, table, or diagram? Why?

Keeping a Portfolio

The more you write, the more ideas you will have. Because you won't write about every idea you have right away, you need a place to keep them. A **portfolio** is a place to keep ideas and bits of information that you might use someday in your writing. You can divide your portfolio into five sections.

1. Getting Ideas

Ideas come from many different places and experiences. You might get an idea from a dream, from talking to a friend, or from a place you have visited. You probably have many more ideas than you have time to write. Save these ideas. You never know when they will come in handy. You can write these on a page in a portfolio. Then, you can come back to them later. Maybe they will help you with your next writing assignment.

2. Prewriting

After you have gone through the prewriting step of the writing process, you should put your work aside for a while. You can do this by putting it in a special section of your portfolio. Also, you can keep copies of your notes, lists, or graphic organizers in this section to keep track of them.

3. Pieces I'm Working On

Drafting and revising are steps that take a while. You should put your writing aside between these steps. You can organize your drafts and revisions in another section of your portfolio. You may want to put them in order by date. That way, you can keep track of the changes you make to your writing.

4. Finished Writing

In this section, you can save all of your completed writing pieces or just the best ones that you want to save.

5. Word List

Are there some words that you always have trouble spelling? Do you sometimes hear a new word that you really like? You can keep a list of words that you use often in this section of your portfolio. That way, you can easily find them when you want to use them.

Making a Portfolio

You will need a three-ring notebook and dividers with pockets.

How to make the pocket dividers

1. Cut a piece of heavy paper that is 9 inches wide and 14 inches long.

2. Fold the paper up 4 1/2 inches to make a pocket. Staple the paper along the edges.

3. Punch three holes in each pocket divider. Put the dividers in the notebook. Put some paper in it, too.

How Does It All Work Together?

Now that Mia had worked through all of the steps of the writing process, she felt much more prepared for her next writing assignment. Her teacher asked her to write about her pet.

STEP 1 Prewriting

Task, Audience and Purpose

Mia's task was to write about her pet. She has a cat named Kit. She decided that her audience would be her classmates. Her purpose would be to either inform or entertain.

Getting and Narrowing Ideas

Mia thought about Kit. She made the following list with the help of her classmates.

	how she behaves
	how she looks
	how to care for her
	where did you get her

Mia asked herself, "What would my classmates be interested in reading about Kit?"

She chose the first three ideas on the list. Mia decided to write a paper that would inform her readers.

Organizing Ideas

Here is the graphic organizer that Mia used.

STEP 2 Drafting

Mia used her graphic organizer to write this draft about Kit.

> My pet is a cat named Kit. She is a calico cat. She has white, black, and orange fur. That makes her a calico cat. She takes good care of her fur so it is very shiney. She w_____ about six pounds.
>
> Kit spends most of her day sleeping in the sun. When I take her outside, she chases butterflies. She also jumps on the backs of people who walk past her favrit tree.
>
> I love Kit so I take very good care of her. I feed her. I play with her. I take her to the vet for a checkup and shots.

Mia put her draft in her portfolio when she was done. She would revise it later.

STEP 3 Revising

Mia read her draft several times. First, she took out extra information. Mia also added words to make some of her sentences more interesting.

My pet is a ^pretty^ cat named Kit. She is a calico cat.

~~She has~~ ^with^ White, black, and orange fur. ~~That makes her a~~

~~calico cat.~~ She takes good care of her fur so it is very

shiney. She w_____ about six pounds.

~~Sometimes she is active and sometimes she isn't~~
Kit spends most of her day sleeping in the sun. When

I take her outside, she chases butterflies. She also jumps

on the backs of people who walk past her

favrit tree.

I love Kit so I take very good care of her. I feed her. ^Before school^ ^After school^

I play with her. ^Once a year^ I take her to the vet for a checkup

and shots.

STEP 4 Editing/Proofreading

Mia used her editing/proofreading checklist. She looked for misspelled words and incorrect punctuation. Mia noticed some mistakes she had made. She marked them with proofreading marks.

My pet is a ^pretty^ cat named Kit. She is a

calico cat. ~~She has~~ ^with^ white, black, and

orange fur. ~~That makes her a calico cat~~ e

She takes good care of her fur^,^ so it is very

shiney.^sp?^ She we **i g h s** about six pounds.

~~sometimes she is active and sometimes she isn't~~
Kit spends most of her day sleeping in the sun. When

I take her outside, she chases butterflies.

She also jumps on the backs of people who walk past her

sp? favrit ^favorite^ tree.

I love Kit^,^ so I take very good care of her. ^Before school^ I feed

^After school^ her. I play with her. ^Once a year^ I take her to the vet for a checkup

and shots.

STEP 5 Publishing

Mia was ready to share her writing with the class. She thought about the best way to do that. She thought it would be fun to make a cat-shaped book. She wrote a couple of sentences on each page in her best handwriting. Then she drew pictures of Kit to go with the words. Finally, Mia checked her book against her edited paragraphs to make sure she hadn't missed anything.

My pet is a pretty cat named Kit. She is a calico cat with white, black, and orange fur. She takes good care of her fur, so it is very shiny.

She weighs about six pounds. Sometimes she is active

Reading Your Writing

Following all of the parts of the writing process will make your writing better. The steps will help you get and narrow ideas and organize your thoughts. They will also help you change, correct, and add to your writing to make it more interesting and easy to read. When you're ready to share your writing with others, the writing process will help you get it ready to publish.

Forms of Writing

This is the part of the Handbook where you can find out how to write letters, reports, stories, descriptions, poetry, and much more. All the different kinds of writing you do are included here, plus some other kinds you may not have tried yet. Are you ready? Then let's get started.

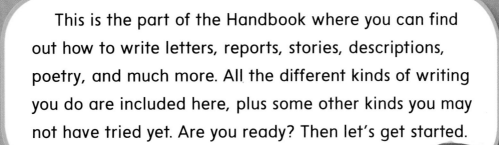

Personal Writing

Do you make lists to remind yourself to do things?

Do you write notes to your friends?

These are examples of personal writing. Look on the next page for more kinds of personal writing you can do.

● ●

Lists and notes are just two examples of personal writing. Other examples of personal writing include the following:

- Self-Reflection Paragraphs
- Journals
- Learning Logs
- Notes and Cards
- Friendly Letters
- Business Letters

EXAMPLE Rita is pet sitting for her neighbor. She lists the jobs she needs to do every day so she doesn't forget anything.

1. feed fish, dog, and cat
2. take dog for a walk
3. brush dog and cat
4. give dog and cat water

Continue reading to see more examples and to find out more information about personal writing.

Self-Reflection Paragraphs

Are your writing skills getting better? You might not know unless you set a goal. Setting a goal gives you something to work toward. It helps you get where you want to go. Let's say your goal is to be a better writer. How will you know when you reach that goal? "Being a better writer" is not specific enough.

To set a specific goal, you have to decide what part of your writing you want to improve. Do you have trouble writing complete sentences? Are your paragraphs a jumble of ideas?

Think about how others have responded to your writing. What have your teachers said about your writing? What notes have you written to yourself in your student journal?

To choose her goal, Erin looked over her papers from second grade. She had also written one paper so far in third grade. Here are some of her teachers' notes:

> ▶ Erin, what kind of house is this? Please tell me more about it.
> ▶ Can you add some adjectives to describe your neighbor?
> ▶ Is this dog tired, playful, jumpy, or scared? Tell your reader!

Erin smiled and nodded. She knew what her writing goal should be for third grade: use more adjectives. She could set that goal and meet it!

EXAMPLE Then Erin wrote about her writing goal. She started each paragraph with a clear topic sentence. Then she added some details. Erin tried to include some adjectives in her writing. She would start working toward her goal right away!

> This year my most important writing goal is to use more adjectives. My writing is too plain now. I need to tell how things look, feel, and sound. Sometimes I can tell how they smell or taste.
>
> For example, when I write about my dog, I won't just say that he is brown. I might write that he has soft, floppy ears and a curled tail that is always wagging. I'll tell how my dog shakes with excitement when he sees me and makes little yipping sounds. Most of the time, he smells warm and furry. When he doesn't, he needs a bath!
>
> When I use more adjectives, my readers will know what I'm talking about. I can paint a clear, interesting picture in their minds. People will want to read what I write!

Try It!

Write down four new writing goals for this school year.

Lists

A **list** is a group of related names, things, or actions. You have probably seen lists for grocery shopping, students in a class, or things a child wants for a birthday gift. The words on a particular list are all about the same subject.

EXAMPLE Here are three different kinds of lists.

Grocery List
milk
eggs
butter
oranges
bread
peanut butter

Mrs. Miller's 3rd Grade Class

Kayla	Mark
Emily	Tyler
Megan	Justin
Julia	Brian
Nikkie	Juan
Amber	David
Mary	Alex
Lauren	Jamal
Diana	Paul

Birthday Wish List
watch
backpack
soccer ball
board game

Reasons for Lists

People make lists for many different reasons. You can make lists to help you remember things, to give more information to others, or to get ideas for writing. There are many different kinds of lists.

Suppose you are planning a birthday party. Writing lists can help you in three ways.

1. **Lists to help remember things**
   List of things to eat (sandwiches, juice, pretzels); List of things to do at your party (play games, face painting, open presents); List of friends to invite to your party (Emily, Tyler, Julia, Juan, Mary, Diana, Paul, Alex)

2. **List to give information to others**
   List of things to write on the invitations (date, time, and place of party)

3. **List to get ideas for writing**
   List of funny things that happened at your party (I wore all the bows from my presents; the dog ran off with the last sandwich.)

Reading Your Writing

Lists are a good way to help you remember things. You can use lists for lots of different things, including grocery lists and information to include on a party invitation. Make sure you include everything on your list, so your readers will have all of the information they need.

Journal

Wouldn't it be nice to write whatever you want and not worry about how it looks or sounds? That's what you can do in a **journal.** It's a place where you can write about anything, in any way you want!

You can write about things that happen to you and how you feel about them. You can write about things you've done and things you want to do. You can write about movies you see or books you read. Your journal is your very own place to write your thoughts about everything.

Soccer practice starts on Tuesday and Cody can hardly wait. He wrote about his favorite sport in his journal.

> **EXAMPLE**
>
> September 22
>
> It's so fun to play soccer! It's the best to be the goalie because you can catch the ball and you can kick it to your teammates. You don't have to do as much work, like running and never getting the ball.

Try It!

Here are some things you could write about in your journal:
- camping with your family
- riding a roller coaster
- a funny thing that happened at school
- a visit to a famous place
- a book you really liked

More About Journaling

People who write books, magazines, and newspaper stories need lots of ideas for their writing. Many authors write in journals. Then they use ideas from their journals to write stories.

Tips for Writing in a Journal

- Don't worry about spelling, punctuation, or neat handwriting. As long as you can read it, that's what matters.
- You can draw in your journal. Sometimes a drawing will give you an idea for a story.
- Try to write in your journal every day. The more you write, the more ideas you will have.

Reading Your Writing

Writing in a journal is a good way to keep track of ideas for your writing. You can write down ideas you don't want to forget and write about them later. The more ideas you have to choose from, the easier it will be to pick a topic that will interest your readers.

Learning Log

A **learning log** is a place where you write about something you are studying. For example, if you are doing a science experiment, you might be watching for changes. You can record those changes in a learning log.

Learning logs can be used for any subject you are studying. You can use charts or drawings in your learning log to help keep track of what you are studying.

Arthur wanted to grow a tomato plant. With his father, he got a pot and filled it with soil. To make a small hole, Arthur pushed his finger into the soil until the dirt reached his first knuckle. Then he put a tomato seed in the hole, covered the seed with dirt, and watered it.

They set the pot with the tomato seed in the sun and watered it every day. Arthur wrote in his learning log whenever he saw changes. Here is part of his learning log.

Growing a Tomato Plant

May 1: Today, I planted a tomato seed in a pot and watered it. I hope the plant will grow lots of tomatoes.

May 9: Something is growing where I planted the seed. It looks like two green petals.

May 30: The plant keeps getting bigger, and now it is growing branches.

June 25: Yellow flowers are growing on the branches! What are they for?

July 3: Green tomatoes are growing where the flowers were. I can't wait to eat them!

Try It!

Sara put up a bird-feeding tray on her back porch. She kept a learning log of the different birds that came to eat. Sara dropped her notebook and the pages of her learning log got all mixed up. Put the pages back in the right order.

Dad helped me hang the tray from a tree. We hope it will keep the pesky squirrels away.

The birds came back! I saw lots of sparrows and finches. There was even a red cardinal!

A squirrel got up on the feeder today. It chased away all the birds!

Today I saw a sparrow. It's the first bird to eat at the feeder!

When you need an idea for writing, read your learning log. The things in your log can be used to write a letter, story, or class report. You record things in the order they happened, so you will be able to write in a clear, orderly way that will be easy for your readers to understand and follow.

Notes and Cards

There are many different kinds of notes and cards. You have probably seen card racks in stores. They have notes and cards for every kind of holiday and event you can think of. There are even cards to wish someone a "Happy Groundhog Day"!

You can buy a card or print one out on a computer. You can also make a card yourself. Add your own personal message and you are ready to send a note or card.

Birthday Card

A birthday card is sent to wish someone a "Happy Birthday." You usually send them before the person's birthday. However, there are special *belated* birthday cards in case you remember the birthday after it is over. Here is the message Eric wrote in a birthday card he made for his grandma.

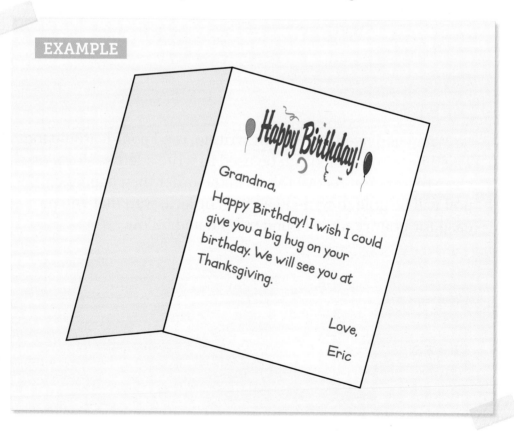

EXAMPLE

Grandma,

Happy Birthday! I wish I could give you a big hug on your birthday. We will see you at Thanksgiving.

Love,

Eric

Get-Well Card

A **get-well card** is sent to cheer up someone who is sick or hurt. Jessica made her friend Ben a get-well card when he was sick with a cold.

EXAMPLE

Hi Ben,

We missed you at baseball practice! Here is a joke to make you feel better. What animal keeps the best time? A watch dog!

See you soon,

Jessica

Get well soon!

Invitation

An **invitation** is a card that asks someone to come somewhere. It should tell the date and time to come and the address where people should go.

You're Invited!

Dayton, Ohio 43012

Come help us celebrate
Danny's 9th birthday!

Date: Saturday, February 5

Time: 2:00 p.m.

Address: 777 Luby Lane
Dayton, Ohio 43012

Thank-You Note

Write a **thank-you note** when you want to thank someone for giving you something or for doing something nice for you. The thank-you note has special information in the *body*. It says thank you and tells why you are thanking the person. Your thank-you note must also have a *greeting, closing,* and *signature.*

Brad wrote a thank-you note to his aunt.

Greeting ▶ | Dear Aunt Jane,

March 16, 2014

Body ▶ | Thank you for letting me come to visit you. I had a great time! I really like the haircut you gave me. The kids in my class think it's really cool.

Closing ▶ | Love,

Signature ▶ | Brad

Try It!

Which kind of note or card would you send for each event below?
- ▶ You are having a Valentine's Day party.
- ▶ Your uncle broke his arm.
- ▶ Your grandpa sent you a basketball.
- ▶ Your friend is having a birthday soon.

Tips for Writing Notes and Cards

▶ Make sure you have spelled the person's name correctly.

▶ Be friendly and polite.

▶ Put commas after the name of the person in the *greeting* and after the *closing: Dear Uncle Bob, Sincerely,*

▶ Decorate your notes and cards with your own drawings and designs.

▶ Remember to include the date, time, and address on invitations.

▶ When you write a thank-you note, be sure to mention the specific gift or assistance you received from the person.

Reading Your Writing

Notes and cards are written for special occasions like birthdays, to let someone know you hope he or she feels better soon, to invite someone somewhere, and to thank someone.

When writing notes and cards, be sure to be friendly and polite. Make sure you have included all of the parts of the note or card you are sending. If you leave something out, your reader will be confused.

Personal Letter

A **personal letter** is a letter you write to a relative or a friend. It's also a letter you write to someone you would like to get to know. Personal letters can be written to a pen pal. They can also be written to a favorite author, actor, actress, or athlete.

Personal letters help you share news, stories, and thoughts. They help you start or continue friendships with people who live far away.

The Parts of a Personal Letter

Heading

The *heading* is your address and the date. The heading goes in the upper right corner of the friendly letter.

Greeting

The *greeting* tells who will receive the letter. Many greetings begin with *Dear,* but you can also use words like *Hi.* Put a comma after the person's name.

Body

The *body* is the main part of the letter. This is where you write the news, stories, and thoughts you want to tell.

Closing

The *closing* lets the person know you are ending the letter. Words like *Love, Your friend,* and *Sincerely* are often used as closings. Be sure to put a comma after the closing.

Signature

The *signature* is your name.

EXAMPLE Grace just moved to Montana. Her best friend
Allie still lives in Kansas. Grace wrote a personal letter to Allie.

Heading ▶

> 853 Mountain View Lane
> Glen Echo, Montana 20812
> September 8, 2014

Greeting ▶ Dear Allie,

Body ▶
Today was the first day of school. It's really
hard to be the new kid in class. One girl
named Mandy was really nice. She has red
hair like you!

You know what's weird? It already snowed! It
didn't snow here in town, just on top of the
mountains. Then it melted.

I haven't seen any moose or grizzly bears yet.
I hope I don't see a grizzly bear.

Guess what! They have soccer here too!
Dad said that I could play. I wish you could be
on my team again.

I miss you so much. Please write to me soon.

Closing ▶
Love,

Signature ▶
Grace

Addressing the Envelope

There are three lines to each **address**.

1. The *person's name* is on the first line. Use the person's first and last names. Be sure to capitalize the first letter of each name.

2. The *house number* and *street name* go on the second line. If there is an *apartment number,* add it after the street name. Capitalize the first letter of each word in the street name.

3. The *city, state,* and *zip code* go on the third line. Capitalize the names of the city and the state. Put a comma between the city and the state. Put a space between the state and the zip code.

Tips for Addressing an Envelope

▶ Put your address in the upper-left corner of the envelope.

▶ Put the address of the person you are writing in the middle of the envelope.

▶ Put a stamp in the upper-right corner of the envelope.

Here is the envelope Grace addressed to her friend Allie.

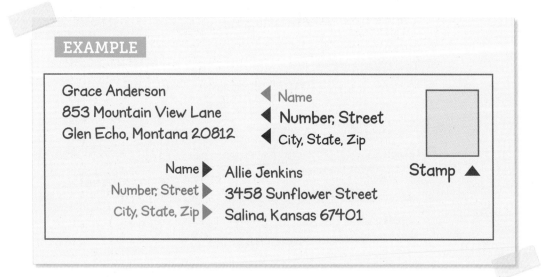

EXAMPLE

Grace Anderson   ◀ Name
853 Mountain View Lane   ◀ Number, Street
Glen Echo, Montana 20812   ◀ City, State, Zip

Name ▶ Allie Jenkins
Number, Street ▶ 3458 Sunflower Street
City, State, Zip ▶ Salina, Kansas 67401

Stamp ▲

Tips for Writing a Personal Letter

STEP 1 Prewriting

▷ List things you've done since you last wrote to the person.

▷ Read your journal for writing ideas.

STEP 2 Drafting

▷ Write your letter. Use your list of new things.

▷ Write as if you were talking to the person.

▷ Write the body of your letter. Then add the other parts: heading, greeting, closing, and signature.

SECTION

2

Forms of Writing

STEP 3 Revising

▷ **Organization** Put all the sentences about the same thing in the same paragraph. Add a topic sentence at the beginning.

▷ **Sentence Fluency** Are sentences smooth and easy to read?

▷ **Voice** Read your letter out loud. Does it sound like you are talking to a friend?

STEP 4 Editing/Proofreading

▷ **Conventions** Look for spelling mistakes in your letter. Be sure your friend's name is spelled correctly! Make sure your friend's name and other proper nouns are capitalized. Check for correct punctuation.

STEP 5 Publishing

▷ **Presentation** Type or write a neat final copy of your letter. Make sure it looks nice and is easy to read.

▷ Address the envelope. Put a stamp on it. Now, mail your letter!

Business Letter

A **business letter** is a serious letter you write to someone at an organization or company for one special reason. It isn't a friendly letter filled with stories and jokes. Some business letters ask that something wrong be fixed. Others request information.

Here are three kinds of business letters and reasons to write them.

1. **A Letter of Complaint** states a problem you have with a product or service offered by a company and asks the reader to fix the problem.

   Suppose you order a paper airplane book. The book company sends you a paper doll book instead. You write a letter of complaint to the book company. You state the problem and ask the company to send the right book.

2. **A Letter of Concern** is written when people are concerned or interested in the same issue. It could be about an issue in your school, your neighborhood, or your city. It's a way of calling the attention of many people to a concern or other idea.

   For example, without special curbs, it's hard for people in wheelchairs to cross streets. You could write a letter to express your concern. You could send it to the newspaper editor to be printed in the paper. If others agree with your concern, your town will begin thinking about making curbs with wheelchair access.

3. **A Letter of Request** asks the reader to send information.

   You think you can break the world record for the most dominoes stacked. You write a letter of request for information on how to get into *The Guinness Book of World Records*.

Checklist for Writing a Business Letter

Use this checklist to make sure your business letters are written properly.

▷ Be serious about your letter. Your reader will be serious about it too.

▷ Be polite. Ask, and don't make demands.

▷ Keep it short. It's easier to keep your reader's interest with a short letter.

▷ "Stick to business." Stay on the subject and you won't lose your reader.

▷ Thank the reader for his or her help.

SECTION

2

Forms of Writing

Try It!

Pick the two letters that are business letters:

▷ a letter to your cousin Bill about coming for a visit

▷ a letter to a toy company asking for its price list

▷ a letter to your friend Liz about the fun you had at the county fair

▷ a letter to a farmer thanking him for having your class visit for a field trip

▷ a letter to the city pointing out the need for more playgrounds in the city parks

Parts of a Business Letter

Heading

The heading is your address and the date. The heading in a business letter goes in the upper-left corner of the letter.

Inside Address

The inside address is the name and address of the person you are writing. The inside address goes between the heading and the greeting. If the person has a title, put a comma after the name and then write the title.

Ms. Carolyn Greenfield, Museum Director

Greeting

The greeting of a business letter is followed by a colon.

Dear Ms. Greenfield:

Body

The body is the main part of the business letter. This is where you write about the problem or ask for information. You don't indent the paragraphs in the body of a business letter.

Closing

The closing goes on the left side of the page, after the body. Words and phrases such as *Sincerely, Sincerely yours,* and *Yours truly* are often used as closings for a business letter. Put a comma after the closing.

Signature

The signature is your handwritten name. If you are using a computer, type your full name four lines below the closing. Sign your name above your typed name.

Jose likes to play with dominoes. His mom read *Guinness World Records 2012.* She told Jose about Alexandr Bendikov's record of 1036 dominoes stacked on one upright domino. Jose practiced stacking dominoes and decided to write a **business letter** to Guinness Media, Inc., for information on how to get into *The Guinness Book of World Records.*

EXAMPLE

174 Cactus Court
Barstow, California 92311 ◀ Heading
January 18, 2014

Guinness Media, Inc.
6 Landmark Square Inside
Stamford, Connecticut 06901 ◀ Address

Greetings: ◀ Greeting
I beat the world record for stacked dominoes. ◀ Body
I stacked 1040 dominoes on top of one
standing domino. That is four more than
Alexandr Bendikov's stacked. I want to be in
The Guinness Book of World Records.
    Please send me the guidelines of how to
get my record into your book. I would also like
a certificate showing that I broke a record.
    Thank you very much.
Yours truly, ◀ Closing
Jose Sanchez ◀ Signature
Jose Sanchez

Checklist for Addressing an Envelope

▷ Write your address in the upper-left corner of the envelope.

▷ Put the address of the person, company, or organization you wrote to in the middle of the envelope.

▷ Put a stamp in the upper-right corner of the envelope.

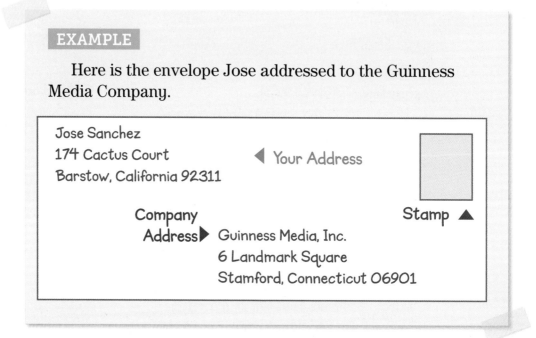

EXAMPLE

Here is the envelope Jose addressed to the Guinness Media Company.

Jose Sanchez
174 Cactus Court
Barstow, California 92311   ◀ Your Address

Company
Address ▶   Guinness Media, Inc.
6 Landmark Square
Stamford, Connecticut 06901

Stamp ▲

Folding a Letter

Fold your letter into three parts. Put your letter into the addressed envelope. Seal the envelope, add a stamp, and mail your business letter!

Tips for Writing a Business Letter

STEP 1 Prewriting

▷ List things you could write about in a business letter. These should include questions, concerns, and complaints.

▷ Read the "Checklist for Business Letters" to help plan your letter.

STEP 2 Drafting

▷ Write your letter. Use your list to help you "stick to business."

▷ Don't worry about neatness or mistakes now. You can make corrections later.

▷ Write the body, and then add the other parts of the letter. Don't forget that a business letter has an inside address.

STEP 3 Revising

▷ **Organization** Make sure you stated the problem, request, or concern; asked for help; and then thanked the reader.

▷ **Voice** Read your letter out loud. It should sound like talking to a grownup you respect. It should be clear and polite.

STEP 4 Editing/Proofreading

▷ **Conventions** Check for mistakes with capitalization. Be sure to capitalize a person's name and title. Don't use exclamation points in a business letter.

STEP 5 Publishing

▷ **Presentation** Write or type a neat final copy of your letter. Write your signature neatly. Address the envelope. Add a stamp. Now, mail your business letter!

SECTION

2

Forms of Writing

Informative Writing

Informative writing does two things. It explains how to do something, or it gives information about something.

Suppose you wrote a report about your favorite animal. Suppose you wrote directions explaining how to make your favorite sandwich. Both are examples of informative writing.

SECTION

2

Forms of Writing

Examples of informative writing include the following:

▶ Summary
▶ Responding to Literature
▶ Responding to Nonfiction
▶ Book Review
▶ Explaining a Process
▶ Giving Directions
▶ News Story
▶ Writing to Inform
▶ Informative Report
▶ Research Report

SECTION

2

Forms of
Writing

EXAMPLE Tory read some paragraphs about
Martin Luther King, Jr. Then she wrote a summary of
what she read.

> Martin Luther King, Jr. was a great American leader. He
> led protests against hate, prejudice, and violence. He was shot
> by James Earl Ray on April 4.

Continue reading to see more examples and to find out
more information about informative writing.

Summary

A **summary** is a short way to explain what you have learned about a piece of writing. You might write a summary after you have read a book, encyclopedia article, or news story or listened to someone else read. A summary should include the main idea and other important ideas of the writing.

EXAMPLE Paul read the following part of "Hot Enough to Fry an Egg" by Raymond Huber.

> Death Valley is probably the most extreme part of the Mojave Desert.
>
> The valley is 140 miles long and is the lowest point in the United States: it is 282 feet below sea level!
>
> It is incredibly dry and hot in Death Valley. In most of the Mojave, temperatures can reach a little over 100 degrees. But in Death Valley, the air temperature can reach 134 degrees Fahrenheit! At ground level it gets up to a sizzling 165 degrees Fahrenheit. That's hot enough to fry an egg!
>
> Death Valley gets less than two inches of rain each year. Parts of the valley floor are covered with a crust of salt. What caused this? Years ago, Death Valley was covered by water. Over time, the area became warmer. When the water began to dry up, it left behind salt and other minerals.
>
> It might seem that nothing could survive in a place called Death Valley, but many animals and plants can. Some, such as the Salt Creek pupfish or the Death Valley monkey flower, are found nowhere else in the world.

Try It!

What do you think the main idea is? What other important ideas would you put in a summary?

EXAMPLE Here is the summary Paul wrote.

> The part of the Mojave Desert that is the most extreme is Death Valley. The temperature at ground level in Death Valley can reach 165 degrees Fahrenheit. Less than two inches of rain fall each year in Death Valley. In addition, a crust of salt covers parts of the valley floor. Even through these extreme conditions, some plants and animals can survive in Death Valley.

Notice how Paul put the main idea in his first sentence. He included four other ideas that he thought were important. Everything Paul wrote about is in the original article. He did not give his opinion. He did not ask any questions. He did not give any new information that was not in the article.

Remember What's Important

Sometimes it is difficult to figure out what the main idea and other important ideas are. You may need to reread two or three times. The things you remember will probably be the most important. You may also get an idea from the title.

Try It!

Now read this information from "Hot Enough to Fry an Egg" by Raymond Huber.

The Mojave Desert is only one desert in the United States. South of it is the Sonoran Desert. It lies in southwestern Arizona, in southeastern California, and in parts of Mexico. This desert covers about 120,000 square miles.

Because it is farther south, the Sonoran Desert has the highest average temperature of the U.S. deserts. Across large portions of the desert, temperatures may rise above 120 degrees Fahrenheit during the day. The nights and winter months are mild. Temperatures seldom drop below freezing.

Which of these sentences should not be in a summary?

The Sonoran Desert is in the United States.

The Sonoran Desert covers about 120,000 square miles.

Temperatures can rise above 120 degrees Fahrenheit.

I would like to visit the Sonoran Desert.

Reading Your Writing

A summary is a quick look at a longer piece of writing. It should tell your reader what the piece is about, without giving too much away. It should be brief and to the point. Be sure to use your own words.

Tips for Writing a Summary

STEP 1 Prewriting

▷ Read the piece of writing carefully.
▷ Write down phrases to answer these questions:
  Who or what was the subject of the book or article?
  What was the main idea about the subject?
  What else is important to my audience?

STEP 2 Drafting

▷ Write your summary using your notes.
▷ Add any ideas you may get as you're writing.
▷ Use your own words. Do not copy from what you are reading.

STEP 3 Revising

▷ **Ideas** Check your prewriting notes. Did you include everything? Did you get the main idea?
▷ **Organization** Get rid of any information that you didn't get from the article.

STEP 4 Editing/Proofreading

▷ **Conventions** Proofread your summary to check for spelling.
▷ **Conventions** Were there any words you couldn't think of that you should fill in now?
▷ **Conventions** Did you indent your paragraph?

STEP 5 Publishing

▷ **Presentation** Write a neat copy. Is it clear and easy to read?

Responding to Literature

Fiction, stories that are made up, has characters, action, setting, and ideas. When you read stories, you try to understand what they are about. You try to understand the roles of the various characters and why they acted as they did. When you write about stories, you are showing what you understand. You are also helping readers have a better understanding of a story.

Try It!

Think of a book you have read.
- ▶ Do you understand why the characters acted as they did?
- ▶ When and where did the story take place? Was that a good setting or not?
- ▶ What happened in the story?
- ▶ What did you think about the ideas in the story?
- ▶ What did the writer want you to learn from the story?

Creating a Web

There are many ways to respond to literature. Lainey just finished reading "A New Life for Mei" by Judy Kentor Schmauss. Lainey decided to respond to the character Mei. She made this web to organize her ideas.

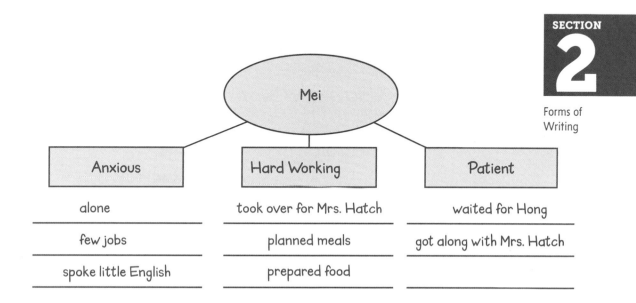

Notice how she put *Mei* in the middle. In each box, she wrote a trait that told about the character. Below each box, she put information from the story to support each trait of the character.

Lainey used the web to write this response to the story. Each paragraph is about one of the traits Lainey thought Mei had. Notice how Lainey wrote a topic sentence for each paragraph. She used information from the web to support her topic sentence.

EXAMPLE

It must have been hard for Mei to leave China and move to the United States. Mei was probably anxious as she and Hong settled in Chinatown. I think she felt alone, especially since she did not speak much English. Also, she could not find a job, so she probably worried about money.

When Mei finally found a job, she seemed to work very hard at her job. Mei took over in the kitchen for Mrs. Hatch when she fractured her arm. Mei planned meals and prepared delicious food. Mei kept the restaurant running smoothly while Mrs. Hatch was away.

I think Mei is patient. When her husband, Hong, is gone for many months working on the railroad, Mei waits patiently for him to return. Also, Mrs. Hatch is moody and a difficult boss, but Mei continues to work hard without complaining.

Try It!

Do you agree with Lainey's analysis of Mei? What other traits could Lainey have included in her analysis?

Tips for Writing a Response to Literature

STEP 1 Prewriting

▶ Decide what qualities you think a character has in a fiction story you have read.
▶ Put your ideas on a web.
▶ Look for information in the story to support each idea. Put it on the web.

STEP 2 Drafting

▶ Use each quality in a separate paragraph.

STEP 3 Revising

▶ **Organization** Do your supporting sentences stay on topic?
▶ **Sentence Fluency** Did you use some long and some short sentences?

STEP 4 Editing/Proofreading

▶ **Conventions** Indent each paragraph.
▶ **Conventions** Make sure you have used capital letters correctly.
▶ **Conventions** Check your response for spelling mistakes.

STEP 5 Publishing

▶ **Presentation** Make a clean copy. Does it look like something you would want to read?
▶ **Presentation** Design a cover for your story. Write your response on the front inside flap.

Responding to Nonfiction

A book can be fiction or nonfiction. **Nonfiction** means that the story or information is about a real person, place, or event. The purpose of nonfiction is usually to inform, explain, or persuade. Sometimes the author of nonfiction has a message he or she wants to give to a reader. When you read nonfiction, you need to keep this in mind.

Whenever you read a book, you have thoughts and opinions about it. These come from your response to the book—what it says or how it says it. When you look through a nonfiction book, you get an idea of whether you are interested in reading it. Whether you know it or not, you are asking yourself these questions: Do I understand the pictures? Are there enough pictures? Do the pictures help me understand the book? Do the headings give me an idea of what the sections will be about? Do the headings sound like something that would interest me? Is the topic important? Is the writer trying to tell me something?

Try It!

What type of nonfiction book would you be interested in reading?

Using a Graphic Organizer

You can understand what you have read better when you write about your reaction. Kylie's teacher asked the class to respond to a nonfiction book. Kylie chose "Storm Chasers" by Alanna Parker. She used this graphic organizer to help her focus as she read.

This book is about

_____

The author wrote this book because

_____

The reasons I think this are

_____

_____

My opinion

_____

I liked/didn't like it because

_____

_____

EXAMPLE Here is what Kylie wrote about "Storm Chasers."

> The nonfiction book "Storm Chasers" is all about people who look for storms. The book gives information about what storm chasers do and why they do it. The photographs and sidebars helped me understand the text.
>
> I think the author wanted to write about storm chasers to tell readers that they do not chase storms only for the excitement, but to tell how they provide information about weather and storms. This valuable information about storms can actually save lives!
>
> I am glad that people are willing to risk their lives to learn more about weather and storms. Chasing storms can be dangerous, but it is worthwhile if it saves lives.

Tips for Responding to Nonfiction

STEP 1 Prewriting

▷ Use a graphic organizer.
▷ Read the book carefully.
▷ Fill in the graphic organizer.

STEP 2 Drafting

▷ Write your ideas down quickly. Use your graphic organizer.

STEP 3 Revising

▷ **Ideas** Is your response to the book clear?
▷ **Organization** Did you answer each part of the graphic organizer?

STEP 4 Editing/Proofreading

▷ **Conventions** Did you spell everything correctly?
▷ Did you capitalize the title?

STEP 5 Publishing

▷ **Presentation** Make a clean copy. Could you add a picture to make it more appealing to your reader?

▷ Share your response with a friend who has read the book. Compare responses.

SECTION

2

Forms of
Writing

FUN fact

In the library, nonfiction books have numbers on the spines.

Book Review

When you write a book review, you are telling others what you think about a book. Reading your review will help them decide if they want to read the book.

Book Review for Fiction

Fiction, stories that are made up, has characters, action, setting, and ideas. For a fiction book, begin by giving the title of the book and the author. Then create a paragraph that gives a short summary. You may want to include **who** the main character is, **what** happened to the character, **when** the story happened, and **where** the story took place. A second paragraph should tell what you thought about the book. You should give reasons for your opinion.

Title: "Little Havana"

Author: Lana Cruce

Summary

Who? a girl named Marisa

What? visiting her aunt and uncle

When? spring break

Where? Miami, Florida

My Opinion: I liked it. It had a happy ending.

EXAMPLE Here is the book report Pilar wrote.

"Little Havana"   ◀ Title
By Lana Cruce   ◀ Author

    A girl named Marisa lives in Minneapolis.
She is going to visit her Aunt Laline and
Uncle Alejandro in Miami, Florida for spring
break. Marisa does not want to go visit them
because she has never met them. When she
arrives in Miami, she is reluctant to learn
about the Cuban culture. Aunt Laline gives
her a costume to wear to a festival called
Calle Ocho, but Marisa chooses not to wear
it. At the festival, Marisa sees everyone
wearing costumes, and she decides to change   ◀ Summary
into her costume.
    I liked this book because it has a happy   ◀ Opinion
ending. Marisa has a good time in Miami and
she is glad she visits her aunt and uncle.
Marisa even learns about the Cuban culture.

Try It!

Did Pilar include all of the necessary details in her summary?
What are your thoughts about "Little Havana?" Do you agree
with Pilar's opinion?

Tips for Writing a Fiction Book Review

STEP 1 Prewriting

▷ Set up a graphic organizer.
▷ Keep *who, what, when,* and *where* in mind as you read the book.

STEP 2 Drafting

▷ Quickly get your thoughts down on paper.
▷ Leave spaces for words you can't think of or can't spell.

STEP 3 Revising

▷ **Organization** Did you pick out the most important things in your summary?
▷ **Voice** Did you make your summary sound as though you enjoyed or didn't enjoy the book?
▷ **Sentence Fluency** Did you use sentences of different lengths?

STEP 4 Editing/Proofreading

▷ **Conventions** Are your paragraphs indented?
▷ Did you underline the title or put the name of the short story in quotation marks? Is it capitalized correctly?

STEP 5 Publishing

▷ **Presentation** Make a clean copy. Is your review easy to read?
▷ Ask your teacher if you can post your book review in your classroom.

Book Review for Nonfiction

Nonfiction means that the story or information is about a real person, place, or event. The purpose of nonfiction is usually to inform, explain, or persuade. Begin with the title of the book and the author. Write a paragraph that tells what the book was about and what you learned from it. Then include a paragraph about what you thought about the book. It is okay if you don't like a book, but you should remember to give good reasons.

Joseph used this graphic organizer for the nonfiction book "Hot Enough to Fry an Egg" by Raymond Huber.

SECTION

Forms of Writing

Title: "Hot Enough to Fry an Egg"

Author: Raymond Huber

Summary: What is it about?

deserts

What did I learn?

many deserts have extreme temperatures

many deserts have extreme levels of rainfall

Death Valley is the most extreme part of the Mojave Desert

Deserts are found on every continent

My Opinion

informative book with good photos

EXAMPLE Here is the book review Joseph wrote for his nonfiction book.

> "Hot Enough to Fry an Egg"
> By Raymond Huber
>
> This book is about deserts and the extreme temperatures and levels of rainfall in deserts. One desert, the Mojave Desert, is a desert that gets extremely hot during the day, but freezing cold at night. The Mojave Desert also has very little rainfall. Death Valley is part of the Mojave Desert, where temperatures can reach 165 degrees Fahrenheit and less than two inches of rain fall each year. The Mojave Desert is just one desert with extreme temperatures. Extreme deserts can be found on every continent.
>
> I learned a lot about deserts from this book. I especially liked the photos because the photos helped me to understand the text.

Reading Your Writing

When writing a book review, your summary is very important. If you tell your readers too much, they will not need to read the book. If you don't tell them enough, they will not want to read the book.

Tips for Writing a Nonfiction Book Review

STEP 1 Prewriting

▷ Use a graphic organizer that will help you focus as you read the book.

▷ Remember to give reasons for your opinion.

STEP 2 Drafting

▷ Get your thoughts down quickly.

▷ Write on every other line so you will have room to make changes.

STEP 3 Revising

▷ **Organization** Did you leave anything out? Check your graphic organizer.

STEP 4 Editing/Proofreading

▷ **Conventions** Did you spell the author's name correctly? Did you capitalize each sentence?

STEP 5 Publishing

▷ **Presentation** Does your book review look easy to read?

▷ Ask your teacher to post your book review on the bulletin board so that other students will be interested in reading the book.

Explaining a Process

When you tell someone how to do something or how to get somewhere, your purpose is to explain. Giving directions or explaining how to do something takes some practice. You must choose your words and write your sentences carefully. It's very important to keep your audience in mind when you explain something. A first grader will not be able to read the same words as an adult. You will also need to use shorter sentences for a first grader. No matter who your audience is, you must use words they will understand. You must explain step-by-step so your reader will be able to follow along.

Putting Things in Order

When you explain a process, you tell someone how to do something. You might explain how to tie a shoe, wash the dog, or wrap a present. To get started, imagine how to do the task in your mind.

Nick thought about how he planted seeds in his garden last summer. Here are the notes he made as he thought about what he had to do.

1. break up the ground
2. make a hole
3. put in the seed
4. cover it
5. water it

Order Words

When you are explaining a process, order words such as *first, next, then,* and *finally* can be very useful. These words will help you keep the steps in the right order. They will also help your reader follow the order better.

Use the following list of order words to signal the correct order of steps when you are explaining a process.

after	first	second
before	last	then
during	next	third
finally	now	while

EXAMPLE Here is the paragraph Nick wrote to tell first graders how to plant a seed. Notice how he used order words.

> Let me tell you how to plant a seed. First, break up the ground. Next, make a hole. Poke your finger into the ground up to your first knuckle. Then, put the seed in the hole. Then, cover it with dirt. Finally, water the seed.

Tips for Explaining a Process

STEP 1 Prewriting

▶ Imagine step-by-step the process you are going to explain.
▶ Write brief notes for each step. You may wish to number them.

STEP 2 Drafting

▶ Write your ideas quickly.
▶ Circle any words you cannot spell correctly or think you will change.

STEP 3 Revising

▶ **Organization** Did you remember all the steps? Are the steps in the correct order?
▶ **Sentence Fluency** Did you use order words to indicate the correct order of the steps?
▶ Ask someone to follow your steps and suggest changes.

STEP 4 Editing/Proofreading

▶ **Conventions** Did you spell all of the words correctly? Did you use good grammar? Remember, you are telling your audience how to do something.

STEP 5 Publishing

▶ **Presentation** Make a clean copy of your work. Can you see any parts that look messy?
▶ Draw a diagram to show what you are explaining.

Giving Directions

When you give someone directions, you tell the person how to get somewhere. You may use words such as *right, left,* and *straight* to clearly explain to your reader. If you are telling someone how to go a long distance, you might also use the word *blocks* or use street names.

To get started, picture a map in your head of the directions you are giving. Imagine you are following the directions yourself. Order is very important. One wrong turn, and your reader is lost!

Chan's mom was coming to help in his classroom. Chan was going to write directions for her. First, he thought about how to get to his room from the front door of the school. This is what he wrote.

turn left

down second hallway

turn right

first hallway

When Chan wrote the directions for his mom, he decided to number them. He thought this would make it easier for her to understand.

> **EXAMPLE**
>
> 1. Go through the front door.
> 2. Turn left.
> 3. Go to the second hallway.
> 4. Turn right.
> 5. Go to the first hallway.
> 6. Turn left.
> 7. My room is the first door on the right. It is C6.

Chan was very specific. He told his mom how many hallways, how many doors, and which way to turn whenever there was a choice.

Try It!

Imagine your grandpa or other family member is visiting your school for the first time. What directions would you give him to get to the office?

Tips for Giving Directions

STEP 1 Prewriting

▶ Picture in your mind the route someone will take, or walk the route if you can.
▶ Make notes as you go.
▶ Write down helpful information, such as what your reader will see along the way.

STEP 2 Drafting

▶ Write your directions quickly while you have the route pictured in your mind.
▶ Cross out or circle words you might change later.

STEP 3 Revising

▶ **Organization** Did you remember all the steps? Are they in the correct order?
▶ **Word Choice** Did you use precise direction words for your audience, such as *left, right, north,* or *south?*

STEP 4 Editing/Proofreading

▶ **Conventions** Are your directions given in the present tense? Did you capitalize each sentence?

STEP 5 Publishing

▶ **Presentation** Make a clean copy of your directions. Are they easy to read?
▶ Draw a map to include with the directions.

News Story

A **news story** is an accurate report about a person or an event that is happening now. The writer must report a news story in a way that makes the reader care about it. Its purpose is to inform readers. A news story should include only facts, no opinions. Readers count on news stories to be accurate and not take sides. Many people form opinions based on news stories, but if the facts are not accurate, readers cannot make the best decisions. For example, a news story might report on a new toy so that parents can decide if it's safe for their children.

News stories should include information that answers the five Ws.

Who?	Who was involved or whom does it affect?
What?	What did he or she do? What happened?
When?	When did the event take place?
Where?	Where did the event take place?
Why?	Why did the person do what he or she did?
	Why did the event happen?

Try It!

Think of something that happened at school recently. Answer the five Ws about what happened.

Parts of a News Story

Here are the parts of a news story.

Heading

This is a title for a news story. It is usually short. It gives the reader an idea of what the article is about in a few words.

Byline

This tells who wrote the news story.

Lead

This is the first paragraph. The five Ws are answered in the lead. This is the part that convinces the reader to read more.

Body

This comes after the lead. Details are given in this part. More information about the five Ws is given in the body. Sometimes people are quoted in this part.

Ending

This finishes the news story. It should not include any new information. It should just be a summary of the news story.

How do you get the answers to the five Ws?

1. **Observation** If you were there, you can report what you saw and heard.
2. **Interviews** If you were not there, you can talk to people who were. **Remember:** a news story must be accurate, so stick to the facts. If someone tells you what he or she thinks, make sure that is clear so readers will know it is not a fact.

Heading ▶

Byline ▶

Lead ▶

Evergreen Third Grader Is Grand Champion

by Kirk Wade

Alicia Gonzales, an Evergreen Elementary third grader, is the grand champion rope jumper from Allen County. Alicia jumped for a record two hours and ten minutes at the North Side Mall yesterday. She raised a total of $600 for her community shelter.

Alicia started training a year ago after reading about the great need for food and warm clothing donations during the winter months at the High Hopes Shelter. She got sponsors through her parents' work and family and friends.

"I am grateful to everyone who supported me and donated to this important cause," Alicia said, after catching her breath. "My parents were very helpful, too. They made sure I ate right and built up my time slowly."

◀ Body

Alicia plans to do this every year, at least until she gets to high school. Then she plans to find another way to help support the shelter.

◀ Ending

Reading Your Writing

Make sure your facts are correct. Don't include opinions. Your news story should inform your reader. Make sure it answers the five Ws.

Tips for Writing a News Story

STEP 1 Prewriting

▷ Do you have the answers for the five Ws?

STEP 2 Drafting

▷ Start with the lead.
▷ Write quickly, getting down all the important facts and information.
▷ Write a headline that lets your readers know the subject of the news story.

STEP 3 Revising

▷ **Organization** Is your story accurate? Did you stick to the facts?
▷ Did you cover the five Ws in the lead?
▷ **Voice** Did you convince your audience they wanted to read your news story?
▷ **Sentence Fluency** Did you tell your news story quickly and simply?

STEP 4 Editing/Proofreading

▷ **Conventions** Check your spelling. If you are unsure of a word, look it up in the dictionary. Check capitalization and punctuation.

STEP 5 Publishing

▷ **Presentation** Make a clean copy of your news story so it is easy to read and appealing to your readers. Publish it in your school or classroom newspaper or submit it to your local newspaper for publication.

Writing to Inform

When you write to inform, use real facts, ideas, or events. One way to organize is by cause and effect. To identify an effect, you ask "What happened?" To find the cause, you ask "Why did that happen?"

Beth was writing a report to explain why frogs lay hundreds of eggs. She knew the effect. She just had to figure out the cause. To help plan her writing, Beth used a graphic organizer.

As Beth read more about frogs, she found that frogs must lay hundreds of eggs to survive. Unlike birds, frogs do not take care of their eggs, so many of the eggs die or get eaten by fish and birds. Now Beth knew how to finish her graphic organizer!

Cause   Effect

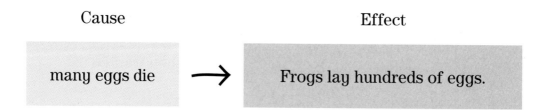

many eggs die → Frogs lay hundreds of eggs.

EXAMPLE Beth liked the cause-effect part of her report. Yet, she saw some details that did not belong. Look at the changes she made below. Her report is much better now!

> Frogs are amphibians. That means they lay their eggs in water. Many kinds of frogs also live part of their lives in water as tadpoles. ~~Snakes are not amphibians because they lay their eggs on land.~~
>
> Frogs are cold-blooded and cannot keep themselves warm. To stay warm in winter, many frogs bury themselves in the mud. ~~I wouldn't want to do that!~~
>
> Frogs have to lay hundreds of eggs because most of their eggs die. ~~Frogs are very bad parents.~~ They do not take care of their eggs, so fish, birds, and other frogs eat most of them.

SECTION

2

Forms of Writing

Informative Report

An informative report can be one page or more. Yet sometimes you need to cover several topics in one report. For example, Henry is going to write about renewable energy. This kind of energy comes from a source that cannot be used up. He wants to cover these topics:

> ▶ solar energy
> ▶ wind energy
> ▶ energy from running water, such as water falling over a dam
> ▶ energy from burning wood and waste products

In Henry's report, each kind of energy will have its own heading. Under each heading, he will write two or three paragraphs. This report may be three or four pages long. It will take careful planning!

Try It!

Think of at least two topics that might be good for a long report. They should include lots of information. Here are some examples to help you get started:

> ▶ how dogs are trained to help people who have trouble seeing or moving around
> ▶ famous people who were born in your state
> ▶ ways that recycling helps the environment

How can Henry organize a long informative report? He can use a web. You can see part of his web below.

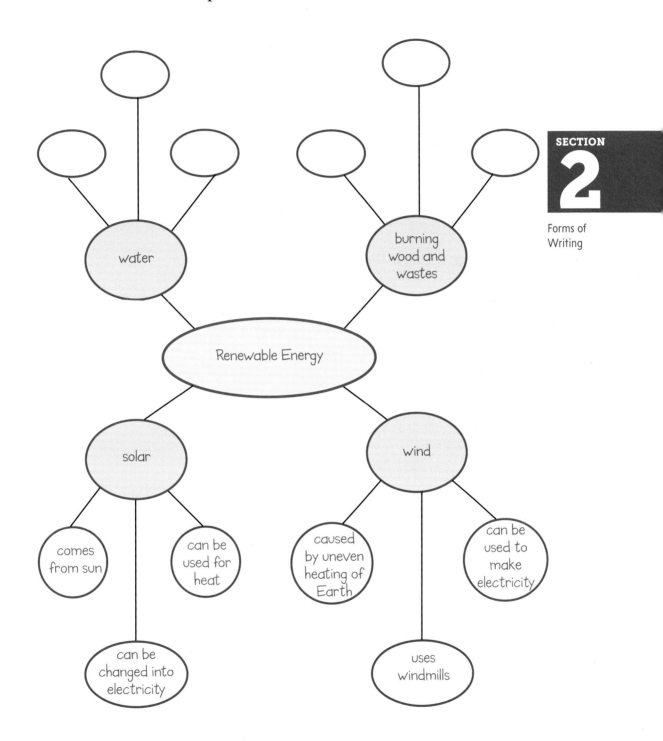

EXAMPLE After Henry made his web, he was ready to write. He would start with a short introduction. It would tell readers what his report was about. Here is the first part of his report:

Title ▶
of the
report

Renewable Energy

Renewable energy comes from the sun, wind, water, and burning wood. We will never run out of those things. Most of the energy we use now comes from oil, gas, and coal. We are running out of those things. This report will tell you about four kinds of renewable energy.

First ▶
Heading

Solar Energy

Solar energy comes from the sun. Solar energy can be used to heat water, homes, and other buildings. Solar energy can also be changed into electricity. Then the electricity can be used to run machines and light up homes. Solar energy from sunny days can be stored. Then we can use it on cloudy days.

Tips for Writing an Informative Report

STEP 1 Prewriting

▶ Choose a topic that interests you. Select one that includes several smaller topics (subtopics).
▶ Gather information on your main topic. Group it into the subtopics.
▶ Use this information to make a web.

SECTION

2

Forms of Writing

STEP 2 Drafting

▶ Use your web to write a draft of your report.
▶ Give each subtopic a heading.

STEP 3 Revising

▶ **Ideas** Are your facts correct?
▶ **Organization** Did you start with a short introduction? Did you group the information into subtopics? Did you stay on the topic under each heading?
▶ **Sentence Fluency** Did you vary the way you began your sentences?

STEP 4 Editing/Proofreading

▶ **Conventions** Did you spell all of the words correctly?

STEP 5 Publishing

▶ **Presentation** Write or print a neat copy of your report.
▶ Add drawings or other pictures if you can.

Research Report

A good way to share what you know or have learned is through a **research report.** The purpose of a research report is to give information about real facts, ideas, or events and explain what you think they mean. The information can be checked by looking in other sources, such as nonfiction books, magazine articles, encyclopedias, newspapers, or the Internet.

A research report:

- ▶ provides information
- ▶ is about real facts, ideas, or events
- ▶ gets straight to the point
- ▶ gives events in the order they happened
- ▶ may be divided into sections by topic, with headings
- ▶ may have photographs, diagrams, or illustrations with captions
- ▶ has information that can be checked in other sources

Try It!

What do you think would make an interesting topic for a research report? How would you gather information about your topic?

Selecting a Topic

Selecting a topic can take some time. Here is what George did as he tried to decide on a topic:

▶ thought about what he was interested in
▶ thought about things he would like to learn more about
▶ talked to his friends
▶ went to the library to get ideas from books

Finally, George decided to write about animals in his home state. He knew he had to narrow his topic because there were too many animals to be able to write about all of them. He thought he would narrow it down to three. He knew he would have to see what he could find in the library before deciding which three.

Gathering Information

The first thing George did was to find a list of the animals in New Mexico. From that list, he chose to learn more about the prairie dog, the roadrunner, and the horned lizard.

George looked for books and encyclopedia articles on each animal. He read each one carefully. George decided he needed additional information about each animal. So, he looked at reliable Web sites on the Internet for more information.

Organizing Information

George wanted to remember what he was reading. He also wanted all the information he gathered to be in one place. Here is how George used a TREE graphic organizer to put the information he gathered in order. In the **T** box, he wrote his topic sentence that told what he was writing about. In the **R** box, he listed three reasons or subtopics. In the **E** box, he further explained each subtopic. In the last **E** box, he provided a good ending that summed up the information about his topic.

T	Topic Sentence: There are many animals in New Mexico.
R	Reason: prairie dog
E	Explanation: small, hairy, short legs and tail, bark
R	Reason: roadrunner
E	Explanation: 20–24 inches, walks or runs
R	Reason: horned lizard
E	Explanation: horns above eyes, changes color, hibernates
E	Ending: many more

Here is George's draft. Notice how each subtopic is a separate paragraph.

There are many animals in new mexico. Some live in the dezert. I will tell you about the prairie dog, the road runner, and the horned lizard.

The prarie dog is small. It is very hairy. It has short legs. It has a short tail. They can bark. Some people keep them as pets. I have a pet cat.

The roadrunner is a big bird. It is about 20 to 24 inches long from its beek to its tail. It cannot fly very well. Most of the time it walks or runs. Roadrunners eat rattlesnakes.

The horned lizard is very scary looking. It has horns above its eyes. It can change colors. Horned lizards hibernate.

SECTION

2

Forms of Writing

Try It!

Read George's draft. Did he include everything from his TREE graphic organizer? Are there additional details he should add? Are there details he should delete?

EXAMPLE Here is George's final draft. Notice the changes he made.

> There are many animals in New Mexico. I will tell you about the prairie dog, the roadrunner, and the horned lizard.
>
> The prairie dog is small and very hairy. It has short legs and a short tail.
>
> The roadrunner is a big bird. It is about 20 to 24 inches long from its beak to its tail. It cannot fly very well, so most of the time it walks or runs.
>
> The horned lizard has horns above its eyes. It can change color so it's hard to see. Horned lizards hibernate during the winter.
>
> The prairie dog, roadrunner, and horned lizard are only three kinds of animals that live in New Mexico.

Try It!

Did George make the changes that you would have made? As George is finalizing his report, what things could he add to his final presentation?

Tips for Writing a Research Report

STEP 1 Prewriting

▷ Choose a topic you know something about or would like to learn more about.
▷ Gather information on the topic.
▷ Put your information in a graphic organizer.

STEP 2 Drafting

▷ Follow your graphic organizer to write a draft.

STEP 3 Revising

▷ **Ideas** Are your facts correct?
▷ **Organization** Do you have a paragraph that introduces your report and one that ends it?
▷ Are your paragraphs organized by topic? Have you stayed on the topic in each one?
▷ **Sentence Fluency** Did you use some short sentences and some longer sentences?

STEP 4 Editing/Proofreading

▷ **Conventions** Did you remember to indent each paragraph? Did you spell everything correctly?

STEP 5 Publishing

▷ **Presentation** Write or type a clean copy of your research report.
▷ Add drawings or photographs if you can.

SECTION
2

Forms of Writing

Narrative Writing

Narrative writing tells a story. The story can be true or make-believe. When you write a story, you are telling your readers what happened. Your story needs a beginning, a middle, and an end. It also needs a setting and characters. Look on the next page for some different kinds of stories you can write.

Examples of narrative writing include the following:

- Personal Narrative
- Writing about a Friend
- Biography
- Realistic Story
- Mystery
- Fantasy Story
- Autobiography
- Trickster Tale
- Tall Tale
- Play

SECTION

2

Forms of Writing

Continue reading this section of the Handbook to find out more information about narrative writing.

Personal Narrative

Good writers often write about what they know best. One of the things you know best is yourself. When you write a story about yourself and your own life, it is called a **personal narrative.**

Think about all the things that have happened to you. How many of the things on the following list have you done?

> ▶ learning to ride a bike
> ▶ going on vacation
> ▶ wishing for a special gift
> ▶ playing with friends
> ▶ moving
> ▶ celebrating a holiday
> ▶ playing sports
> ▶ exploring
> ▶ participating in a contest

You could write a personal narrative about any one of the items on the list. You should choose something that was important to you. Maybe it was something you thought was exciting or maybe you learned something. If you can remember clearly what you thought about something, it will be easier to write about it.

Try It!

If you had to write about one event in your life, what would it be?

Creating a Graphic Organizer

It is important to help your reader feel involved in your writing. When you describe your feelings, the setting, or the situation well, your reader gets caught up in the story.

SECTION

2

Forms of Writing

EXAMPLE Here is a graphic organizer Steven used to plan his personal narrative about the first time he rode in an airplane.

What Happened	How I Felt	◀ Beginning
vacation	excited	
What Happened	How I Felt	◀ Middle
up early	tired	
plane late	impatient	
plane ride	excited	
What Happened	How I Felt	◀ End
visit with Grandma	happy	

The beginning of your personal story must get the reader interested. The middle should tell all about the event. The ending should wrap things up for the reader.

EXAMPLE Here is Steven's personal narrative.

> This summer my mom and dad told me we were taking a plane to see Grandma. I had never been on a plane. I was very excited.
>
> We left early in the morning. I was very tired. They told us at the airport our plane was late. I didn't want to wait.
>
> When we got on the plane, I sat next to the window. I saw houses, cars, and even mountains. It was really neat.
>
> Finally we were there. I ran into Grandma's arms and she gave me a big hug. We had a nice visit.

Reading Your Writing

Your personal narrative should be about something that really happened in your life. Make sure you stick to your topic.

Tips for Writing a Personal Narrative

STEP 1 Prewriting

▷ Think of a meaningful event in your life.
▷ Use a graphic organizer to help organize your thoughts.
▷ Write down what happened and how you felt.

STEP 2 Drafting

▷ Write your thoughts quickly.
▷ Follow your graphic organizer carefully.

SECTION

2

Forms of
Writing

STEP 3 Revising

▷ **Organization** Does your beginning pull the reader in?
▷ **Voice** Can your reader tell what you were feeling?
▷ **Sentence Fluency** Did you use variety in your sentences or did you start them all the same way?

STEP 4 Editing/Proofreading

▷ **Conventions** Did you indent each paragraph?
▷ Do you have any run-on sentences or fragments?

STEP 5 Publishing

▷ **Presentation** Make a clean copy. Does your work look inviting?
▷ Add photographs or illustrations.

Writing about a Friend

Think of a special friend. How would you describe this person? Let's say your friend is a girl. You could tell how tall she is and the color of her hair and eyes. You might say that she is in your class at school or lives down the street. These details are important, but they do not help your readers get to know your friend.

You do want to tell how your friend looks. Then your readers can start to picture her in their minds. Describing her clothes might help show what kind of person she is. Telling where she lives and goes to school is important, too.

Yet to help readers really get to know your friend, you need to tell what she likes and dislikes. What is her favorite thing to do? What would she never do? What would she like to do, if she got the chance? Would she rather watch a movie or play a sport? Can she speak another language? What other special thing can she do?

To begin, make some notes about your friend. That's what Corey did before he wrote about his friend Sam:

looks a lot like me
loves to play computer games
not such a hot soccer player
quiet until you get to know him
makes me laugh
shares his lunch when I forget mine
invites me on his family campouts

Then Corey organized his description into three paragraphs. First, he told what Sam looks like. Then he told what Sam likes and dislikes. Last, he told why he likes Sam. Corey started each paragraph with a topic sentence. Then he added details in each paragraph.

My friend Sam does not look unusual. He is as tall as most third graders. He has light brown skin and dark brown eyes. His curly hair is always cut short, and he wears glasses most of the time.

Sam is kind of quiet, but you soon find out what he likes and does not like. For example, he hates soccer. "Too much pushing and shoving," he says. Yet Sam loves computer games. His parents had to set strict rules about how long he could play computer games every day. Last month, Sam spent all of his birthday money on a great new game.

I like to play computer games with Sam, but we would be friends even without computers. I can always count on him to make me laugh or share his lunch when I forget mine. Last summer, I went on a fun camping trip with Sam and his dad. Whenever I remember how hot, tired, and hungry we got, I smile. I love to spend time with Sam. He is my best friend!

Biography

Writing about the life of a real person is called a **biography.** Anyone can be the subject of a biography. The person may be alive today or have lived in the past. Often, a biography is about the life of a person who has done important things or made a difference, but it doesn't have to be. Any person can be the subject of a biography. All that you need is a person to write about and an audience to read it.

A biography is different from a story because everything and everyone in a biography is true and real. A biography is different than an informational report because a biography is organized in the order things happened in the person's life.

SECTION

2

Forms of Writing

Try It!

Name two people whose biographies you would like to read or write.

What Makes It a Biography?

A biography:

- is about a real person's life, written by someone else.
- gives important information about a person's life.
- tells what the person did, said, and thought.
- may be about the person's whole life, or just an important part.
- is often told in the order events happened.

SECTION

2

Forms of Writing

What Is in a Biography?

A biography may include:

- the dates of a person's birth and death.
- the person's family history.
- important events in the person's life.
- quotes from the person.

Gathering Information for a Biography

Because a biography is a true story about a real person, you must learn about the person before you can write about him or her. How can you do that?

Interviews

SECTION

2

Forms of
Writing

If the person is alive, you may talk to him or her, or others who know that person. You may also talk to someone who used to know the person.

Sample Interview Questions
▶ What are some of your earliest memories?
▶ What was it like growing up in your family?
▶ What advice do you have for students today?

Research

You can look in newspapers, magazines, or encyclopedias or search Websites on the Internet if the person is famous. Then, take notes on what you read, using your own words. Write down the title of each source you use.

You Should Look For
▶ dates
▶ important events
▶ works or deeds

It takes a lot of time and research to write about a person's entire life. You may want to write about just a short time period or one or two important events in the person's life.

Creating a Time Line

Sofia decided to write about the Brothers Grimm. She reread an article about them that she had read in class. Sofia decided that the best way to organize her information was with a time line.

Date:	1785	1786	1796	1798
Event:	Jacob born	Wilhelm born	their father dies	moved to Cassell to go to school

1812		1859	1863
Nursery and Household Tales published		Wilhelm dies	Jacob dies

Sofia's time line starts with the birth of the brothers. Her time line ends with the death of the brothers. Events on the time line are in the order they happened.

Try It!

What does Sofia's time line tell you about the Brothers Grimm?

Narrative Writing · Biography   135

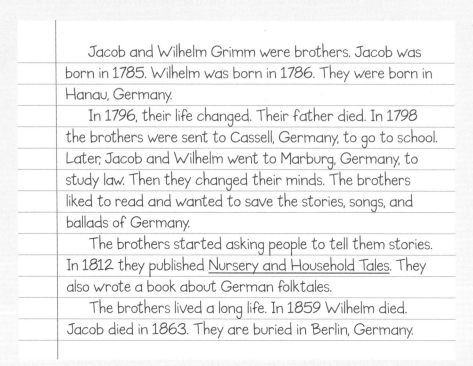

EXAMPLE Here is Sofia's biography of the Brothers Grimm.

Jacob and Wilhelm Grimm were brothers. Jacob was born in 1785. Wilhelm was born in 1786. They were born in Hanau, Germany.

In 1796, their life changed. Their father died. In 1798 the brothers were sent to Cassell, Germany, to go to school. Later, Jacob and Wilhelm went to Marburg, Germany, to study law. Then they changed their minds. The brothers liked to read and wanted to save the stories, songs, and ballads of Germany.

The brothers started asking people to tell them stories. In 1812 they published <u>Nursery and Household Tales</u>. They also wrote a book about German folktales.

The brothers lived a long life. In 1859 Wilhelm died. Jacob died in 1863. They are buried in Berlin, Germany.

Tips for Writing a Biography

STEP 1 Prewriting

▷ Think of someone you admire and think others will as well.

▷ Interview that person or do research to learn more about him or her.

▷ Take notes on your graphic organizer.

SECTION

2

Forms of
Writing

STEP 2 Drafting

▷ Write your thoughts down quickly.

STEP 3 Revising

▷ **Organization** Are the events in the order in which they happened?

▷ **Word Choice** Did you choose descriptive words to write about the person and their important events?

STEP 4 Editing/Proofreading

▷ **Conventions** Did you spell the name of the person correctly?

▷ Did you use quotations correctly?

STEP 5 Publishing

▷ **Presentation** Make a clean copy in the form of a book.

▷ Add photographs or illustrations.

Realistic Story

A **realistic story** contains people, places, and events that are made up, but could be real. A story about a boy who wants a puppy for his birthday would be realistic. The boy and the puppy are not real, but they seem real.

When you write a realistic story, you use your imagination to write a story that entertains your audience. Your story can have funny characters, exciting places, or strange events that could be true. That's what makes it different from a fantasy. In fantasy, things happen that could never really happen.

Try It!

Which of the ideas below could you use to write a realistic story?
- Two friends try out for a team.
- A girl meets a singing turtle by a pond.
- Your neighbor's dog wins the spelling bee at school.
- A boy gets a brand-new bicycle for his birthday.

Parts of a Realistic Story

A realistic story has a plot, one or more characters, and a setting. The plot of a realistic story has events that could happen in real life. The characters act like real people or animals would. The setting is a place that is real or could be real.

Putting the "Real" in Your Story

The "real" in your story begins with an idea. Details of your ideas make the characters and events come to life.

You can get many ideas for realistic stories from things and places around you. Something at school may give you an idea. An event in your neighborhood or town can get you started.

The idea for the example on the next page came from an event at Josh's school. Every year his school has a Games Day. Josh decided to use this event for his story. Although he made up the story, he wanted it to seem real. Josh added details to make his character, Nate, seem real. He made Nate nervous before the race. He also made Nate dream of winning a blue ribbon. With his idea and details, Josh made Nate seem like a real person. You can do the same thing in your stories.

Try It!

▶ While you're reading Josh's story, ask yourself if the characters, setting, and events are realistic.

▶ Pay attention to the details in Josh's story that make it realistic.

EXAMPLE Here is a realistic story that was written by Josh.

Nate got to school early on Friday morning. He was excited about Games Day. Nate saw his friend Brad on the playground.

"Are you nervous?" asked Brad.

"A little," said Nate.

Nate was one of the fastest runners in third grade. Today he might win a blue ribbon. He had a dream about winning a blue ribbon.

It was time for the race. The runners lined up. At the signal, they all started to run.

Nate got a good start, but Tina was ahead of him. He thought about the ribbon. He ran faster and faster. He passed Tina and crossed the finish line. He won!

Later, Nate walked home. He looked at his blue ribbon. He smiled and thought, "I guess dreams do come true, sometimes."

Tips for Writing a Realistic Story

STEP 1 Prewriting

▶ List some things you have done.
▶ List some places you have been or would like to visit.
▶ List some interesting people you have known.
▶ Choose a setting, some events for your plot, and the characters for your story.

STEP 2 Drafting

▶ Write your realistic story. Use your notes.
▶ Don't worry about mistakes. You can correct them later.

STEP 3 Revising

▶ **Ideas** Could your setting be a real place?
▶ Do your characters act real? If they don't, change how they act and what they say.
▶ **Sentence Fluency** Are your sentences smooth and easy to read?

STEP 4 Editing/Proofreading

▶ **Conventions** Proofread for spelling mistakes.
▶ If you have written dialogue, make sure the punctuation is correct.

STEP 5 Publishing

▶ **Presentation** Make a neatly typed or written final copy.

SECTION

2

Forms of Writing

Mystery

A **mystery** occurs when something happens and how or why it happened is not clear. The person who solves the mystery is called a detective. Two famous fictional detectives are Sherlock Holmes and Nancy Drew.

Imagine this: Fred left his library book on the kitchen table. When he went to get it an hour later, it was gone. Where could it be? Now you have a mystery.

SECTION 2

Forms of Writing

To write a mystery, you can begin with a problem. Perhaps something is missing. Maybe something has been damaged, or something has appeared. Then you give clues so your readers can solve the mystery. Sometimes there are clues that do not help. These are given to throw the reader off track. They make the reader think about other solutions for the mystery.

EXAMPLE Below are some possible solutions to the mystery of Fred's missing library book.

> Mom left the house about half an hour ago. Maybe she took the book back to the library.
>
> The dog ran off with it. He is curious and always takes things off the table.
>
> Fred left it somewhere else. He is very forgetful.

Try It!

Think of another possible solution to the mystery of Fred's missing library book.

Parts of a Mystery

Like other stories, a mystery has characters, a setting, and a problem in the plot. The plot must have a crime or a mysterious happening. One of the characters has to solve the mystery. Clues are also part of the plot in a mystery. Clues are hints that might help you solve the mystery. The clues do not tell you the answer.

Suspense and Surprise

SECTION

2

Forms of Writing

You can use suspense and surprise in your mystery. They keep your readers on the edge of their seats. **Suspense** is when your reader isn't sure what will happen next. **Surprise** is when something sudden or unexpected happens.

Here's an example of suspense.

Where could Fred's book be? He couldn't afford to pay for the missing book. What will he do?

This is an example of surprise.

When Fred opened the closet door, hundreds of books fell to the floor.

EXAMPLE Here is the beginning of Fred's mystery.

Fred was always reading. He walked around all day with a book in his hands. One day Fred left a library book on the kitchen table. When Fred went back to get the book, it was gone.

Where could the book be? He couldn't afford to pay for the missing book. What will he do?

Fred looked all over for the book. Then he noticed his bookmark on the floor near the rocking chair. Fred went over to investigate. Yes, it was his bookmark all right.

Fred yelled for his sister. "Rita, have you seen my book?"

"Was it the one about planes?" asked Rita.

"Yes. Have you seen it?" Fred said.

"Nope, haven't seen it," Rita answered, a little too quickly.

Tips for Writing a Mystery

STEP 1 Prewriting

▶ Think of a problem and several possible solutions.
▶ Plan clues that lead to one of the solutions.
▶ Use a graphic organizer to plan characters, setting, a problem, clues, and a solution.

STEP 2 Drafting

▶ Write your mystery.
▶ Follow your graphic organizer.

SECTION

2

Forms of Writing

STEP 3 Revising

▶ **Word Choice** Do your words add suspense to the mystery?
▶ **Voice** Does the personality of your detective come through?
▶ **Organization** Do your clues add up? Do they lead to a solution?

STEP 4 Editing/Proofreading

▶ **Conventions** Have you indented each paragraph?
▶ If you used dialogue, did you punctuate it correctly?

STEP 5 Publishing

▶ **Presentation** Make sure your mystery looks neat and is easy to read.

Fantasy Story

A **fantasy** is a story that has characters, places, or events that could not exist in the real world. Maybe the characters act in a way that is impossible. Is it possible for a carpet to fly? Is it possible for animals to talk or for rain to turn to meatballs? Is there such a place as the Land of Toys? Are elves, unicorns, and hobbits real? All of these things are possible in a fantasy story.

A fantasy story is different from a realistic story. In a realistic story, the characters, setting, and events in the plot could be real but are not. In a fantasy, there might be some things that seem real, but there will be many other things that couldn't be real.

SECTION

2

Forms of
Writing

Try It!

Think about the books you have read or the stories you have heard. Which ones were fantasies?

Reading Your Writing

When you write a fantasy story, make sure the events follow a logical order. Watch out for spelling and punctuation mistakes.

EXAMPLE Lee had to write a fantasy story for homework. He looked around his room to get ideas. Here is the first part of Lee's fantasy story.

One morning, on a very gray day, Oswald woke up feeling kind of strange. He stretched his fins, yawned, and looked around. Across the room, he saw his fish tank. His boy was in it! Sleeping! The boy who always came to feed him, change his water, and talk to him was in his tank. Sleeping!

Oswald got up to get a closer look and was surprised to find out that he could actually walk. His fins were moving just like feet. He walked across the room to his fish tank. He looked in. Just then his boy yawned, stretched, and woke up.

Narrative Writing • Fantasy Story   147

What's So Special about Fantasy?

Look carefully at the chart below. It shows what might be in a fantasy. When you write a fantasy, you may wish to include one or more of these things. You do not have to include all of them.

What is in a fantasy story?

▶ People, animals, and things that have powers they don't have in the real world
▶ Events that could not happen in the real world
▶ Places that do not exist
▶ Creatures that do not exist

Examples:

▶ Disappearing people, talking elephants, flying cars
▶ A rainbow in the dark, boats sailing on clouds
▶ A place where you never grow old
▶ Unicorns and elves

Try It!

Look back at Lee's fantasy to answer this question.
   Which events were not possible?

Tips for Writing a Fantasy Story

STEP 1 Prewriting

▶ Look for a story in your portfolio that you could make into a fantasy.

▶ Think of which element or elements of fantasy you want to include. Think about how you will include them.

STEP 2 Drafting

▶ Write on every other line so you will have space to make changes later.

STEP 3 Revising

▶ **Organization** Do you have a good beginning, middle, and end?

▶ **Sentence Fluency** Have you used some long and some short sentences?

STEP 4 Editing/Proofreading

▶ **Conventions** Proofread for spelling.

▶ Have you capitalized proper nouns?

STEP 5 Publishing

▶ **Presentation** Make a clean copy and illustrate it.

▶ Consider putting it in your portfolio or making it into a puppet show or play.

Autobiography

When a writer writes about his or her own life, the book is called an **autobiography.** An autobiography is about a real person and real events. Everything in it is true.

An autobiography is often written by someone who is famous, but it doesn't have to be. Anyone can write about his or her own life. Most of the time, autobiographies are written in the order that events happened in the person's life.

Some people write about their childhood. Some people write about special times in their lives when they did or saw something important. Still others write about their whole lives up to the time they began writing.

How can you tell you are reading an autobiography? The words *I*, *me*, *my*, and *myself* are good clues.

Try It!

Name a favorite writer whose autobiography you would like to read.

What Makes It an Autobiography?

An autobiography:

tells about the life of the person who wrote it.
is about a real person and real events.
is often told in the order that events happened.
uses words such as *I, me, my,* and *myself.*

What Is an Autobiography?

An autobiography may include:

the date and place that the author was born.
information about the author's life.
events that other people remember about the
    author's early childhood.
events that the author remembers.
photographs and drawings.

Try It!

Which of these ideas could you use to write your autobiography?
- Vicki sang a solo at the concert.
- The boy lost his dog.
- I live in Charlotte, North Carolina.

Gathering Information for an Autobiography

Suppose you were going to write an autobiography. You would be writing about your own life. Most of the information you need is right in your own mind!

Family Interviews

There are some things you cannot remember about yourself. What were things like when you were born? What were you like when you were very little? To find out more about these things, interview your parents, grandparents, aunts, uncles, and even your older brothers and sisters.

Research

Doing research about yourself will help you remember things you might have forgotten. Look through old photos. Look for stories and journals you wrote. Can you find letters and birthday cards people sent you?

Think About:
▶ what you would like to tell people about your life
▶ your favorite things and memories
▶ what it was like growing up on your street

Choose important people, places, and things that happened in your life to write about. Certainly your birth is important! Describe where you live and what your family is like. Write about things you like to do. The more details you add, the more interesting your autobiography will be to read.

Creating a Web

Billy thought about the autobiography he was about to write. He decided that the best way he could organize his ideas was to use a web.

SECTION

2

Forms of Writing

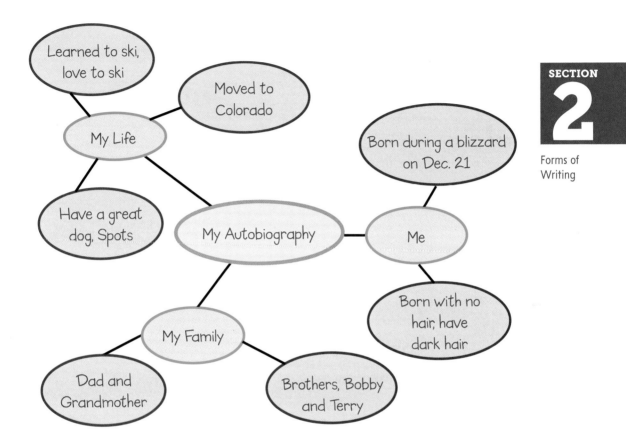

Billy's web is filled with short notes. When he writes his autobiography, he will use the notes to help him remember what he wants to write about.

Try It!

Look at Billy's web. What things will he write about?

EXAMPLE Here is Billy's autobiography.

I was born on December 21, the shortest day of the year. I was born during a blizzard. When I was born, I was bald. Now I have black hair just like my father.

I live with my father, my two brothers, and my grandmother. We moved from Des Moines, Iowa, into my grandmother's house in Boulder, Colorado, last fall. My brother Terry is the oldest. My brother Bobby is the youngest. I am right in the middle.

Last winter my brothers and I took skiing lessons. Learning to ski was difficult. Every time I fell, my dog Spots came up and licked me on the face. Now, I love to ski. My grandmother says that I love to ski because I was born during a blizzard.

Try It!

Read Billy's autobiography. Did he include everything from his web? Follow Billy's example to write your own autobiography.

Tips for Writing an Autobiography

STEP 1 Prewriting

▷ Interview people who knew you when you were very little.
▷ Think about what you would like people to know about your life.
▷ Look at things you made and read when you were younger. Look at photographs.
▷ Jot down notes on your graphic organizer.

SECTION 2

Forms of Writing

STEP 2 Drafting

▷ Put your notes into sentences. Get your thoughts on paper quickly.
▷ Make notes about illustrations and photos you may add.

STEP 3 Revising

▷ **Adding Detail** Did you add details to your sentences?
▷ **Organization** Is it clear when events happened? Does their order make sense?
▷ **Sentence Fluency** Are your sentences clear and easy to read?

STEP 4 Editing/Proofreading

▷ **Conventions** Does each sentence end with the correct punctuation?
▷ Do all the proper names begin with capital letters?

STEP 5 Publishing

▷ **Presentation** Write a neat copy of your autobiography.
▷ Add photographs and illustrations. Add captions.

Trickster Tale

A **trickster tale** is similar to a folktale. A folktale is an old story that teaches a moral, or lesson, about life or explains how something came to be. Originally, folktales were stories that were told as part of an oral tradition. Eventually, these stories were written down.

Trickster tales have tricksters or foolish characters, as well as wise characters. The trickster plays jokes, does tricky things, or tries to convince other characters to do what the trickster wants. Sometimes these sneaky pranks backfire and the trickster is tricked. The good, less foolish characters usually win out in the end. The good characters teach the moral of the tale.

Try It!

Think about folktales you have read. Were there any trickster characters in those stories?

What Tricksters Are Like

Trickster characters:

- are usually animals, most often spiders, rabbits, and coyotes.
- have human qualities. They can talk and tell stories.
- are clever and think of ways to outsmart others.
- are sometimes foolish, silly, and funny.
- often play jokes or pranks on others.
- often can change what they look like.

SECTION

2

Forms of Writing

What Makes It a Trickster Tale?

In some trickster tales, the story explains how something came to be. For example, the book *Grandmother Spider Brings the Sun* explains how the sun came to the dark side of the world. It tells how the tricksters, Coyote, Possum, and Big Bad Buzzard, fail on their mission to steal a piece of the sun while the good, wise character, Grandmother Spider, succeeds. The story also explains why the possum has a hairless tail and how the buzzard became bald.

Before You Begin

Before you begin to write your trickster tale, read some folktales with a trickster character or some trickster tales to study what they are like. You might read trickster tales, such as *Grandmother Spider Brings the Sun* by Geri Keams, *Coyote: A Trickster Tale from the American Southwest* by Gerald McDermott, or *Zomo the Rabbit: A Trickster Tale from West Africa* by Gerald McDermott.

Notice that trickster tales explain something special. When you are trying to decide what to write about, you might think of what is unusual or special about an animal or a place. Ask yourself questions such as, "Why does a rabbit have long ears?" "How did sharks get their fins?" "How is a rainbow made?"

Before you begin your trickster tale, look around you. You might get ideas from a tree, or the sky, or a lake. How did it get there? What is special about it?

Try It!

When you are thinking about a topic, think about things such as:
   Why doesn't a snake have legs?
Remember: Use your imagination!

Creating a Story Map

Sasha is writing a trickster tale about how the elephant got its trunk. She is using a story map to help her do her prewriting. A story map is a graphic organizer.

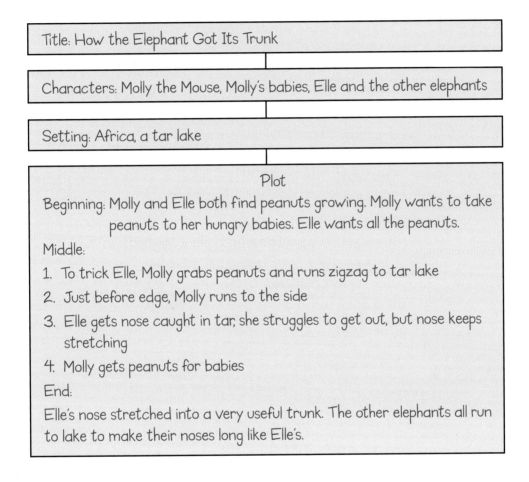

Title: How the Elephant Got Its Trunk

Characters: Molly the Mouse, Molly's babies, Elle and the other elephants

Setting: Africa, a tar lake

Plot

Beginning: Molly and Elle both find peanuts growing. Molly wants to take peanuts to her hungry babies. Elle wants all the peanuts.

Middle:

1. To trick Elle, Molly grabs peanuts and runs zigzag to tar lake

2. Just before edge, Molly runs to the side

3. Elle gets nose caught in tar, she struggles to get out, but nose keeps stretching

4. Molly gets peanuts for babies

End:

Elle's nose stretched into a very useful trunk. The other elephants all run to lake to make their noses long like Elle's.

EXAMPLE Here is the beginning of Sasha's trickster tale.

The Elephant's Trunk

Molly the Mouse was hunting for food for her babies. She found peanuts growing in the dirt. As she was about to take some, someone shouted, "Don't touch those peanuts!" Molly turned to see Elle the Elephant. Elle had huge ears, white tusks, and a pig's snout nose. Staring down at Molly, Elle boomed, "Those peanuts are mine!"

"I'll only take a few," Molly said.

"You won't take any!" Elle answered.

"What should I do?" Molly thought. Then she got an idea. She said, "Just try and catch me!" She grabbed a peanut in her mouth and began to run in zigzags toward a lake filled with brown, sticky tar. Elle chased after her.

Right before Molly got to the edge of the lake, she made a quick turn. Elle ran right into the lake, face first. She was stuck!

Tips for Writing Trickster Tales

STEP 1 Prewriting

▶ Read trickster tales to study what they are like.
▶ Use a story map to plan your trickster tale.

STEP 2 Drafting

▶ Use the notes in your story map as a guide.
▶ Write your draft, getting your ideas quickly on paper.

SECTION

2

Forms of
Writing

STEP 3 Revising

▶ **Ideas** Do you have a beginning, middle, and an exciting ending? Does your ending make sense?
▶ **Word Choice** Do your words describe your characters? Do your words describe the action and plot of the story?

STEP 4 Editing/Proofreading

▶ **Conventions** Did you capitalize the words in your title?
▶ Did you capitalize the characters' names?
▶ Did you indent each paragraph?
▶ Did you use correct quotation marks and commas?

STEP 5 Publishing

▶ Make a neat final copy of your trickster tale.
▶ Illustrate your trickster tale.

Tall Tale

A **tall tale** is a made-up story that usually exaggerates or stretches the truth. It includes unlikely events or problems and creative solutions. The main character usually isn't real. Tall tales are often funny and usually larger than life. A tall tale is different from a realistic story. Not everything in a tall tale could be real.

Have you ever read a story about Paul Bunyan, John Henry, Pecos Bill, or Shorty Long? They are all characters in tall tales.

SECTION

2

Forms of
Writing

FUN fact

Some people say John Henry was a real person who helped build a railroad tunnel in West Virginia between 1870 and 1873.

Try It!

Think of an exaggeration for one of the following situations.

▶ what happened to your homework
▶ what will happen if you eat peas
▶ a fish you saw over the weekend

Parts of a Tall Tale

Like a realistic story, a tall tale has one or more characters, a setting, and events in a plot. In some tall tales, characters, settings, and events might seem as if they could be real, but there is something about them that is hard to believe. Other tall tales are not believable at all, such as the sun crying or a wolf singing.

When you are planning what you will write about, think about exaggeration, unlikely situations or problems, and creative solutions. Think of situations you have been in, things you have read about, or people you have known. Then, try to exaggerate them. Talk to your friends and write down any ideas they have for characters, unlikely events, or solutions.

SECTION

2

Forms of
Writing

Here is a tall tale that Kelsey wrote after reading several tall tales on her own.

Amelia was a character. No one knows where she came from or how old she was. What people do know is that Amelia was the fastest and strongest person around. She was so quick she could run faster than lightning. She was so strong, she could pick up a horse with one hand.

She wasn't just fast and strong. It seemed like Amelia was always helping people out, without even being asked. One day, the people of Big Gulch, Oklahoma, needed help in a big way. A telegram had come saying that a runaway train was going to hit Big Gulch General Store.

It didn't take Amelia long to figure out what to do. She went out of town to where the train tracks ran near a cotton field. She pulled up the tracks and headed them into the field.

That train came along and followed those tracks right into the field. It slowed down in the soft cotton and finally stopped. Not one person got hurt, thanks to Amelia's quick thinking. Everybody was so thankful, they made Amelia the sheriff of Big Gulch.

Getting Started

Writing a tall tale isn't easy. It took Kelsey a long time to do her prewriting. She had to think hard about what she wanted Amelia to be faster than. She thought of all kinds of fast things before she decided on lightning.

Kelsey has made a good start. She can put her tall tale in her portfolio and add to it later.

SECTION

2

Forms of Writing

Try It!

Read Kelsey's tall tale. What details would you add? What would you have had Amelia be faster than?

What Makes a Tall Tale a Tall Tale

Here are definitions for the parts of a tall tale and examples of how those parts were used in the book *John Henry* by Julius Lester.

Exaggeration

Something is made out to be bigger or more than it is.

Example: John Henry grew so big the day he was born that his head went through the porch roof.

Unlikely Event or Problem

An event or problem that couldn't really happen.

Examples:

Event: A rainbow wrapped itself around John Henry's shoulders.

Problem: A huge boulder in the road could not be broken with dynamite.

Creative Solution to a Problem

A good way of solving a problem that couldn't really be done.

Example: When a boulder couldn't be broken up by dynamite, John Henry broke it up with his two sledge hammers and finished building a road at the same time.

Tips for Writing a Tall Tale

STEP 1 Prewriting

▶ Look through your portfolio for ideas.
▶ Talk to your friends.
▶ Make notes on characters, setting, problem, and solution. Use a graphic organizer.

STEP 2 Drafting

▶ Put your notes into sentences quickly.
▶ Circle any words you might want to change later.

STEP 3 Revising

▶ **Voice** Does it sound as though you enjoy the characters and events you are telling about?
▶ **Word Choice** Are your words helping your readers imagine the character, setting, and events?

STEP 4 Editing/Proofreading

▶ **Conventions** Make sure your verb tense is the same throughout your tall tale.
▶ Capitalize proper nouns and the names of special places, such as rivers and mountains.

STEP 5 Publishing

▶ **Presentation** Make a clean copy in the form of a tall book.
▶ Put your tall tale in your portfolio so you can add more later.

Play

A **play** is a story that is written to be performed in front of an audience. The writer of the play tells the story by writing what the characters do and say.

Like a story, a play has characters, a setting, and events in the plot. The characters are the actors in the play. They may be people or animals. The setting in a play is also called the scene. It is where the action takes place and when it takes place. When you tell where and when the story takes place, you are setting the scene.

A play is different from a story or report. Stories and reports are written to be read. A play is written to be performed. A play has stage directions, lines, and props. Stories and reports don't have them.

SECTION

2

Forms of
Writing

Try It!

Imagine you are writing a play about your classroom. Name three characters. Set the scene.

Parts of a Play

Imagine this play: It is the first day of school. The teacher is Mr. Dawes. The students are talking and laughing when the bell rings. The examples that follow each definition below are based on this play.

Stage Directions

These are the directions that tell the characters where to move or how to speak. These are given in parentheses so the performers know it is something to do, not say. They are often in italics. You can do this if you write your play on a computer at school.

Example: (The bell rings and the students go to their seats.)

Lines

These are the words spoken by the characters. The speaker's name is at the beginning of the first line. It is written with all capital letters and followed by a colon.

Example:

MR. DAWES: Good morning, class. I am your new teacher, Mr. Dawes.

Props

Props are objects that will be used by the actors and sounds that are made offstage. These are part of the stage directions.

Example: a bell ringing, desks and chairs for Mr. Dawes and students

EXAMPLE Kay's play is based on the story of the three little pigs. First, Kay listed the characters and the important events in the order they happened. Then, she wrote the dialogue for each character. Finally, she went back and filled in stage directions.

Here is the beginning of Kay's play.

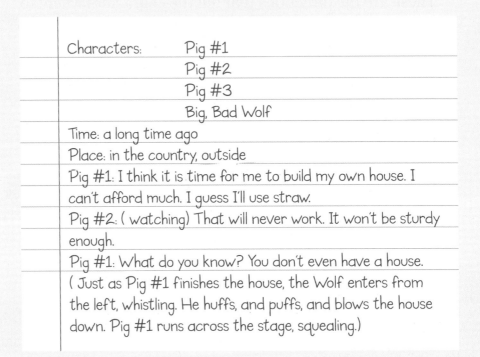

Characters: Pig #1
                Pig #2
                Pig #3
                Big, Bad Wolf

Time: a long time ago

Place: in the country, outside

Pig #1: I think it is time for me to build my own house. I can't afford much. I guess I'll use straw.

Pig #2: (watching) That will never work. It won't be sturdy enough.

Pig #1: What do you know? You don't even have a house.

(Just as Pig #1 finishes the house, the Wolf enters from the left, whistling. He huffs, and puffs, and blows the house down. Pig #1 runs across the stage, squealing.)

(Pig #2 is building a house of sticks. Pig #1 runs up to him. Pig #2 doesn't seem to notice that Pig #1 is out of breath.)

Pig #1: Well, you were right about my house. A big, bad wolf came along and blew it down. Can I live with you?

Pig #2: I hate to say I told you so, but I did. You can stay for a while.

(The pigs finish building the house and go inside. The wolf enters and speaks to the audience.)

Wolf: Watch this, I'll get two for the price of one. (He looks toward the house of sticks, cups his hands around his mouth, and yells.) Oh, little pig, could I borrow a couple of apples? I'd like to make a pie. I'll share it.

Pig #2: (bravely) Go away! I don't have any apples.

Wolf: That's not very nice. Let's try this again. Let me in (getting angry) or I'll huff, and I'll puff, and I'll blow your house down!

Try It!

Read Kay's play. Then find three other classmates to act out the play.

What Makes a Play a Play

Writing a play takes planning and attention to details. A writer has to decide what characters will say and how they will move on the stage. These details are written as stage directions and dialogue.

What the characters say and the way they say it lets the audience know what each character is like. For example, the wolf starts to sound angry. He doesn't have much patience, and he isn't very nice.

How the characters move also helps us understand them. After the wolf blew down Pig #1's house, the pig ran away squealing. We know that he was afraid.

SECTION

Forms of
Writing

Try It!

Look back at Kay's play.
 ▶ Count how many times Pig #1 speaks.
 ▶ Read the stage directions aloud.
 ▶ What props will Kay need for this play?

Reading Your Writing

Keep in mind when you write your play that it will be acted out. Your dialogue and stage directions need to make the play come alive.

Tips for Writing a Play

STEP 1 Prewriting

▷ Choose a story you already know.
▷ Develop your stage directions and dialogue based on what will happen in your play.

STEP 2 Drafting

▷ Write what each character in your play will say.
▷ Add stage directions.

STEP 3 Revising

▷ **Organization** Do your stage directions go with the action that is taking place?
▷ **Ideas** Did you include the most important events from the story you used?

STEP 4 Editing/Proofreading

▷ **Conventions** Did you remember to put the characters' names at the beginning of their lines?
▷ Did you put parentheses around the stage directions?

STEP 5 Publishing

▷ **Presentation** Make a neat copy of your play. Make a cover with the name of the play on it.
▷ Practice and perform your play. Use real people and costumes or puppets.

SECTION

2

Forms of Writing

Descriptive Writing

Descriptive writing gives a clear picture to your readers. It helps your readers see what you see. It helps them hear what you hear. It helps them feel what you feel. The following section will give you tips on writing good descriptions.

SECTION 2

Forms of Writing

Types of descriptive writing include the following:

- Describing a Setting
- Describing a Character
- Describing a Plot
- Describing an Experience
- Comparing and Contrasting Events
- Comparing and Contrasting Places
- Comparing and Contrasting Experiences

Continue reading this section of the Handbook to see examples and to find out more information about descriptive writing.

SECTION

2

Forms of
Writing

Writing a Description

A **description** gives details about a person, place, thing, or action. Descriptions create pictures in the minds of readers by telling what you see, hear, feel, smell, or taste. Good descriptions make your writing clearer and more interesting.

SECTION

2

Forms of Writing

EXAMPLE Read this descriptive writing from "The Country Mouse and the City Mouse" by Vidas Barzdukas. What are some of the descriptive words he used?

Country Mouse gave her cousin a tour of the farm. They visited green pastures and a pond surrounded by purple and yellow lilacs. City Mouse sat down on a rock and smiled contentedly.

"It sure is quiet and peaceful here," City Mouse remarked. "What do you do for excitement?"

"I do lots of things!" Country Mouse answered. "I watch the clouds and listen to the birds sing. I count the number of croaks from the bullfrogs in the pond. Sometimes I collect colorful leaves all day long!"

Using Senses in a Description

EXAMPLE Haley found a surprise on the table when she came home from school. She decided to write a description about it.

> When I got home from school, I saw a rose on the table. It was my favorite color, dark red! It smelled better than the perfume my mom wears. I touched a petal. It was soft and silky. The rose was in a smooth glass vase. It had lots of water in it for the rose to drink. Then I saw a little card beside the vase. It said, "Haley, I love you! Dad." My first rose!

Try It!

Read Haley's description. List some of the descriptive words she uses. Would you have used different descriptive words?

Organizing a Description

A good **description** uses many senses to describe something. Tell your reader how things look, sound, feel, taste, and smell. You give readers great pictures in their minds when you use several senses to describe things.

A good description is organized. Good organization helps hold your reader's attention. A *top-to-bottom* graphic organizer is one way to organize the details of a description.

Look again at Haley's description. She used a *top-to-bottom* graphic organizer to put the details in order. What details did she put at the top of her organizer? What details did she use in the middle? Finally, what details were at the bottom?

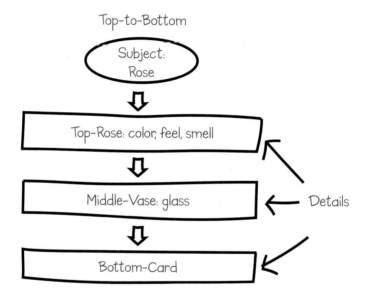

Top-to-Bottom

Subject:
Rose

Top-Rose: color, feel, smell

Middle-Vase: glass   Details

Bottom-Card

Reading Your Writing

Descriptive writing gives details about a person, place, thing, or action. It uses the senses to create a picture in the mind of the reader.

Tips for Writing a Description

STEP 1 Prewriting

▷ Read your journal to get ideas of what to write.
▷ Use a top-to-bottom graphic organizer to get your details in order.

STEP 2 Drafting

▷ Write your description using your graphic organizer.

SECTION

2

Forms of Writing

STEP 3 Revising

▷ **Sentence Fluency** Make sure you don't start all your sentences the same way.
▷ **Word Choice** Do your descriptive words create a picture in your reader's mind?

STEP 4 Editing/Proofreading

▷ **Conventions** Be sure to put commas in lists of three or more adjectives.
▷ Use a dictionary if you are not sure of the spellings of your descriptive words.

STEP 5 Publishing

▷ **Presentation** Make a neat final copy of your description. Check for eraser marks.

Describing a Setting

The setting is an important part of a story. It includes where and when a story takes place. The setting is part of a good book review. If a book is about a hurricane, write about the wind, the rain, and also where the hurricane came to shore. If a story takes place during a war, explain how it may have affected the story.

As you describe a setting, be brief. Yet you can add a few important details to help readers picture the story. Michael wrote the draft below as part of his book review. He began with a good topic sentence. Then he added details about the story.

EXAMPLE

> The story "Little Havana" was written by Lana Cruce. Most of the story takes place in Miami, Florida. Marisa goes there to visit her aunt and uncle. When she arrives in Miami, she does not want to learn about the Cuban culture. Her aunt gives her a costume to wear to a festival called Calle Ocho, but Marisa chooses not to wear it. At the festival, Marisa sees everyone wearing costumes, and she decides to change into her costume.

Then Michael read his draft. He knew he should add more details about the setting of the story. To give additional details about where the story happened, he decided to tell more about Miami, Florida.

EXAMPLE Look at how Michael revised his draft. He added details about the setting. He added other details to make his writing clearer. These details improved his review.

The story "Little Havana" was written by Lana Cruce. Most of the story takes place in Miami, Florida. Marisa goes there to visit her aunt and uncle. When she arrives in Miami, she sees buildings that are painted pink, yellow, and orange. She also sees the bright, blue ocean. Marisa smells spicy food and hears Latin music. At first, she is reluctant to learn about the Cuban culture. Her aunt gives her a ruffled yellow costume to wear to a festival called Calle Ocho, but Marisa chooses not to wear it. At the festival, Marisa sees everyone wearing beautiful, elaborate costumes. She feels sad that she hadn't worn her costume. She changes into her costume and is glad she had come to visit.

Try It!

What are some words you could use to describe the city where you live?

Descriptive Writing · Describing a Setting   181

Describing a Character

You are writing a book review. The book is fiction, so it has made-up characters in it. You want to tell about some of these characters.

Did you read "Writing about a Friend" on pages 130–131? Writing about a character is something like writing about a friend. You need to tell how each main character looks. You need to tell how that character fits into the story, too. For example, two boys might be brothers.

Your friends are nice people, so you write nice things about them. Yet some of the characters in a story might be selfish or lazy. They might tell lies. When you are writing about characters in a story, you need to tell the good and the bad about them.

Characters show what they are like by what they say, what they do, and how they treat other people. Read your book again. This time, take notes on the character you plan to describe. For example, Robert read "The Three Little Pigs." He took notes on the wolf. Then he organized his notes into this web.

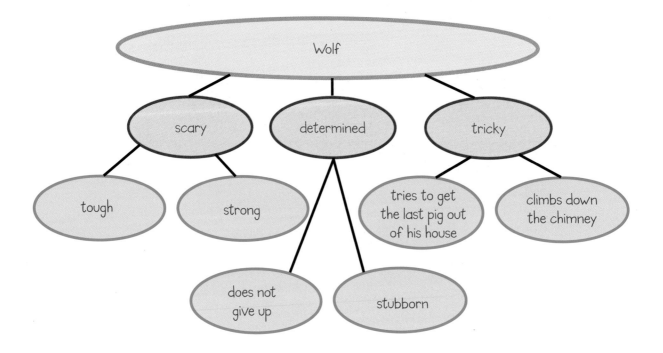

EXAMPLE Robert used his web to write about the wolf. He wrote a paragraph for each medium circle. He started each paragraph with a topic sentence. Then he added descriptive details.

    I liked the wolf in "The Three Little Pigs". He was scary, tough, and strong, strong enough to blow down houses.

    The wolf was determined. He did not give up when he could not blow down the last pig's house. He was stubborn—and hungry.

    The wolf was tricky, too. He tried several ways to get the last pig. For example, he tried to trick the pig into meeting him at a turnip field. Also, the wolf tried to slip down the pig's chimney. That didn't work, but it did show that the wolf was a scary, determined, tricky character.

Describing a Plot

When you write about a fiction book, you should describe its plot. That is, you need to explain the main events in the story. Of course, if it is a mystery, be sure not to give away the ending. You do not want to spoil the story for your readers!

Look at the graphic organizer below. It can help you describe a plot. First, you tell about the problem that one or more characters face. Maybe a family on a boat ride sees storm clouds ahead. Then the problem gets worse. The wind picks up, and waves send water spilling into their boat. They try to call for help on their cell phones, but the phones will not work so far from shore.

Next, tell how the problem is solved. Perhaps a bigger boat nearly runs over the family's boat in the storm. Just in time, someone spots the smaller boat and the scared, wet family. Last, tell how the story ends. Maybe everyone promises to check the weather report before the next trip!

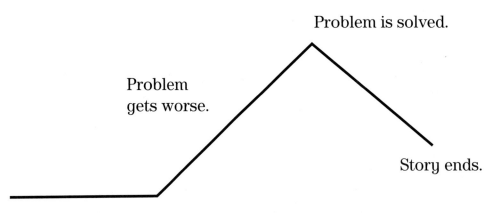

Problem is solved.

Problem
gets worse.

Story ends.

Problem is explained.

EXAMPLE Kayla used this graphic organizer to explain the plot in a book she read. She wanted to tell just the main events. Still, she tried to include interesting details. You can read part of her report below.

I read "A New Life for Mei" by Judy Kentor Schmauss. It begins with Mei and Hong leaving China to start a new life in California. Hong finds a job on the Transcontinental Railroad, but has to leave Mei in order to work. At first, Mei is nervous about being alone and finding a job. She finally finds a job at a restaurant at a hotel. Mei works hard and enjoys her job. Although Mei is a good worker, her temperamental boss fires her, and Mei has to look for another job. Mei thinks about moving to another place in California, but the hotel owner gives her a job. He even makes her the manager and head chef at the restaurant. At the end, Hong returns and Hong and Mei are glad they are starting a new life in America.

Try It!

Read Kayla's story. Then identify the different plot elements in her story. Identify the problem, how the problem is solved, and how the story ends.

Describing an Experience

It can be fun to share your experiences with others. A cause-effect graphic organizer can help you plan this kind of writing. In the cause box, you tell what happened to you. In the effect box, you tell how you felt about it. You might also tell what you did about it.

For example, Iris wanted to write about moving to her new town. You can see how she filled in her graphic organizer.

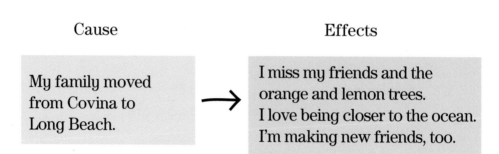

Cause

My family moved
from Covina to
Long Beach.

Effects

I miss my friends and the
orange and lemon trees.
I love being closer to the ocean.
I'm making new friends, too.

Like Iris, you might have many effects to write about. Still, using this kind of graphic organizer can help you think of them. Iris wrote a paragraph for each effect. You can read her first draft on the next page.

In July, my family moved from Covina to Long Beach. Both of my parents have new jobs in Long Beach. That's how I ended up at Miller Elementary School.

The move caused many changes in my life. I really miss the lemon and orange trees in Covina. Still, I love to go to the beach here and watch the waves crash on the shore.

I miss my old friends in Covina, too, especially Julie, who lived next door. Yet I am making new friends here. I just tried out for softball. I made the team, so I have a whole group of friends already!

Reading Your Writing

Using descriptive words helps your reader better understand your writing. Make sure to use words that help the reader see, hear, feel, smell, or taste things you write about.

Comparing and Contrasting Events

Some reports compare two events. To write this kind of report, choose two events that are the same in some ways and different in others. For example, it would be hard to compare the Gold Rush in 1849 with the San Francisco earthquake in 1906. These events were both in the past. They both took place in California. Yet they were very different. They were too different to compare in a report.

After you choose two events, gather facts about them. You might find facts in library books. Check an encyclopedia, too. An adult might help you search on the Internet. Write each fact you find on a note card.

A Venn diagram can help you organize these facts. Look at the next page. Lee used this Venn diagram to compare and contrast two events from the past. One event was traveling west by wagon. The other was traveling west by train. In each circle, he told about one event. That showed how the events were different. Look at the overlapping part. There, Nate wrote ways that both events were the same.

Try It!

Think of two events that you could compare and contrast. For example, you might write about your first day in second grade and your first day in third grade. You could tell how these two days were alike. Then you could explain how they were different.

Traveling from the East Coast to California

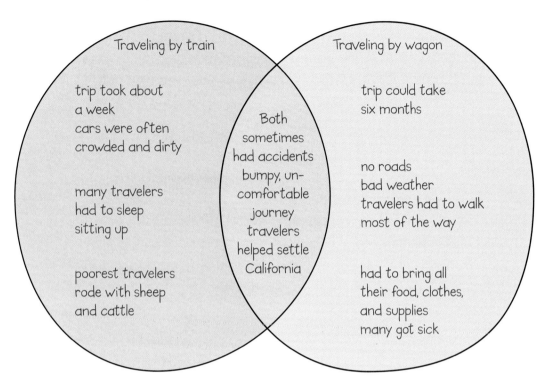

Traveling by train

trip took about
a week
cars were often
crowded and dirty

many travelers
had to sleep
sitting up

poorest travelers
rode with sheep
and cattle

Both
sometimes
had accidents
bumpy, un-
comfortable
journey
travelers
helped settle
California

Traveling by wagon

trip could take
six months

no roads
bad weather
travelers had to walk
most of the way

had to bring all
their food, clothes,
and supplies
many got sick

SECTION

2

Forms of
Writing

Nate also made a time line. It shows the main events in the order that they happened.

Date	Event
1841	First wagon travels to California.
1848	Gold is discovered in California.
1855	First railroad tracks cross the Mississippi River.
1869	Railroad tracks from the East join tracks from the West in Utah. Now trains can cross the nation.

Descriptive Writing · Comparing and Contrasting Events   189

EXAMPLE Nate began his report with a short introduction. It told what his report was about. He used facts from his timeline to write it. He added transition words to help explain what happened when. You can read his introduction below:

> People first began taking long wagon trips west in 1841. Then gold was found in California in 1848. After that, people rushed to the West. Most rode in wooden wagons. By 1869, a railroad stretched from coast to coast. Soon many people began taking the train to travel to the West. This report compares traveling by wagon and by train. Which do you think was better?

Tips for Comparing and Contrasting Two Events

STEP 1 Prewriting

▷ Choose two events that interest you. Select two that are the same in some ways and different in others.
▷ Gather information on both events.
▷ Use a Venn diagram to organize your facts.

SECTION

2

Forms of Writing

STEP 2 Drafting

▷ Use your diagram to write your first draft.
▷ Start with a short introduction.
▷ Tell how the two events are the same.
▷ Then tell how they are different.

STEP 3 Revising

▷ **Ideas** Are your facts correct? Did you explain the facts clearly?
▷ **Organization** Did you use transition words (first, then, next) to help show the order in which events happened?

STEP 4 Editing/Proofreading

▷ **Conventions** Make sure your sentences are all complete. Indent each paragraph.

STEP 5 Publishing

▷ **Presentation** Write or print a neat copy of your report.
▷ Add drawings or other pictures of both events, if possible.

Comparing and Contrasting Places

Some reports tell how two places are alike and different. For example, you might compare and contrast two parks. If you just moved, you might compare your old school and your new one.

Mary Kate loves the mountains. She wanted to tell how the Sierra Nevada and the Coast Ranges are the same and different. First, she wrote down some things she knew about the mountains. Then her dad helped her find a Web site about them. Mary Kate took notes from it, too.

Then she organized her notes into the outline below. Mary Kate will add more details before she starts writing.

SECTION

2

Forms of Writing

I. Sierra Nevada
   A. 500 miles long and up to 15,000 feet high
   B. largest mountain range in CA
   C. includes the Mount Shasta Volcano
II. Coast Ranges
   A. 800 miles long and about 4,000 feet high
   B. makes two climates
      1. much rain on the west side
      2. little rain on the east side
      3. different crops are grown on each side
III. How they are the same
   A. fun to hike in
   B. beautiful to see

Mary Kate added more facts to her outline. Then she used the outline to write the following report.

The Sierra Nevada are huge. They stretch for 500 miles. The mountains are 7,000 to 15,000 feet high. Some of the peaks are covered with snow all year. Mount Shasta Volcano is part of this mountain range. Its last real eruption was around 1800.

The Coast Ranges are 800 miles long. However, these mountains are small. Most of them are less than 4,000 feet high. Still, they affect our climate. They stop many storm clouds coming off the Pacific Ocean. The clouds drop rain on the west side of the mountains. Evergreens grow well there. The east side is much drier. Grapevines and fruit and nut trees grow well there.

I love these ranges. My family has fun hiking in them. Every time we go, we find another beautiful place!

Comparing and Contrasting Experiences

Nate's teacher has asked his class to write about a special experience. Nate thinks about last fall. He went hiking with his older brother in the Coyote Hills Regional Park. They walked along the Muskrat Trails Loop. The boys spotted some amazing birds and other animals in the marshes. The skies were filled with hawks. Nate had a great time.

Then Nate remembers going hiking with his parents along the Tidelands Trail. It had marshes, too, but it ran along part of the San Francisco Bay. That was fun! Nate decides to write about both hiking trips. He will tell how his experiences on these two hikes were the same and different.

To begin, Nate lists things he remembers about each trip. He does not just tell about what he saw. He also explains how he felt about both experiences. Then he organizes his notes into two webs. You can see them on the next page.

Try It!

Think of two experiences that you could compare and contrast. For example, you might write about getting a new puppy and getting a new baby sister. You could tell how these two experiences were alike. Then you could explain how they were different.

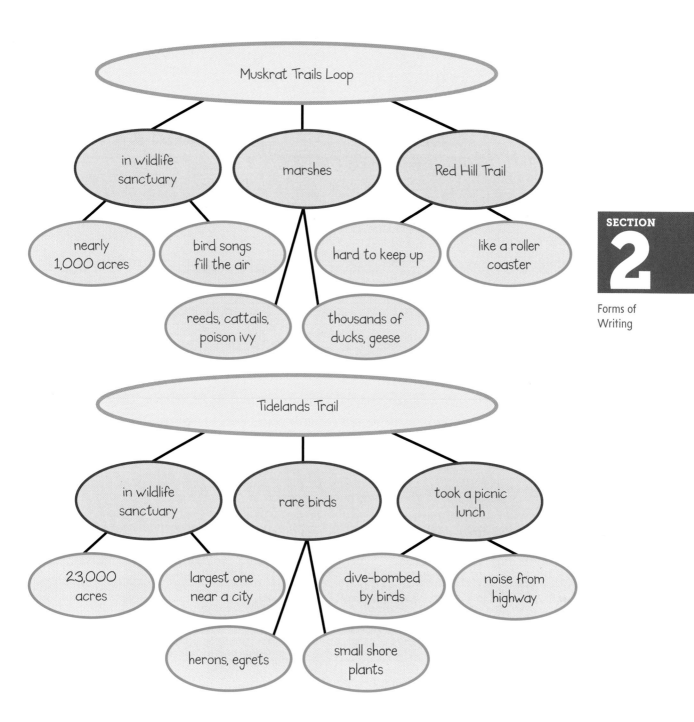

Muskrat Trails Loop
- in wildlife sanctuary
  - nearly 1,000 acres
  - bird songs fill the air
- marshes
  - reeds, cattails, poison ivy
  - hard to keep up
  - thousands of ducks, geese
- Red Hill Trail
  - like a roller coaster

Tidelands Trail
- in wildlife sanctuary
  - 23,000 acres
  - largest one near a city
- rare birds
  - herons, egrets
  - dive-bombed by birds
  - small shore plants
- took a picnic lunch
  - noise from highway

Nate used his webs to tell about each hiking trip. Then he told how the two trips were the same and different. Read it on the next page. Do you see how he used transition words, such as *first* and *later*? They help show the order in which things happened.

EXAMPLE

I had a great time on both trips. They were both wildlife sanctuaries, although Tidelands was in a much bigger park. I saw thousands of birds and ducks. Tidelands had more shorebirds, such as egrets and herons, since we were right by the San Francisco Bay.

Hiking with my brother was hard. At first, he waited for me, but later he kept telling me to hurry up. I think he was trying to wear me out, especially on the steep Red Hill Trail. My parents walked slower and stopped at least every half hour.

My brother and I just had some water and snacks with us, but my parents brought a picnic lunch. Peanut butter sandwiches never tasted so good!

Tips for Comparing and Contrasting Two Experiences

STEP 1 Prewriting

▷ Choose two interesting experiences. Make sure they are the same in some ways and different in others.
▷ Take notes about both experiences. Include facts and your feelings. You could use two webs to organize both sets of facts.

SECTION

2

Forms of Writing

STEP 2 Drafting

▷ Use your webs to write your first draft.
▷ Start with a short introduction.
▷ Tell about both experiences.
▷ Then tell how they were the same and different.

STEP 3 Revising

▷ **Voice** Can readers tell how you felt about both experiences?
▷ **Organization** Did you use transition words (*first, then, next*) to help show the order in which events happened?
▷ **Word Choice** Did you add descriptive details?

STEP 4 Editing/Proofreading

▷ **Conventions** Do you have any run-on sentences or fragments?

STEP 5 Publishing

▷ **Presentation** Write or print a neat copy of your report.
▷ Add photos of both experiences, if possible.

Opinion Writing

An opinion is the way you think or feel about something. Opinion writing does two things. It lets readers know what you think about something. It can also try to persuade, or make, readers do something.

· ·

SECTION

2

Forms of
Writing

Opinion writing lets the reader know how you think or feel about something. You can write an opinion paragraph to express your opinion. Opinion writing can also try to get a reader to act in a certain way. This is called persuasive writing. Types of persuasive writing include a persuasive paragraph, a persuasive letter, advertising, and even a cereal box design.

Try It!

Below are two good reasons to support the importance of studying. Can you think of another good reason?

▶ It helps you learn.
▶ It helps you get good grades.

Continue reading this section of the Handbook to see examples and to find out more information about opinion writing.

Opinion Paragraph

One way to express your opinion is to write a paragraph that tells the reader the way you think or feel about something. Because an opinion is what YOU think, it can't really be wrong, especially if you have reasons for your opinion. Most opinion paragraphs have three parts: the *topic sentence, body, and ending sentence.*

SECTION

2

Forms of
Writing

1. The *topic sentence* tells the reader what the subject of the paragraph is. It also tells your opinion—this is called the "writer's viewpoint"—about the subject.

2. The *body* of an opinion paragraph gives the reasons and facts to support your opinion. At least three reasons should be included, and the most important reason is often given last.

3. The *ending sentence* should summarize the reasons and opinion.

Choosing a Topic

Choose a topic that you feel strongly about. Ask yourself, "Why is this important to me?" Think about your readers. Will this topic be important to them, too?

Try It!

What topic do you feel strongly about? Think about why the topic is important to you.

Sharing Your Opinion

You should use certain words and phrases to express your opinion. Phrases such as the ones below can help you state your opinion.

Opinion Words

▶ I think …
▶ I feel …
▶ I like…/I don't like …
▶ My favorite part is …
▶ This book is so …

Sharing Your Reasons

You should always include at least three reasons, or facts, to support your opinion. Reasons help the reader understand why you feel or think a certain way. Use linking words such as the ones below to connect your opinion and reasons.

Linking Words

▶ Because
▶ Therefore
▶ Since
▶ For example
▶ One reason
▶ Another reason

Reading Your Writing

Make sure you support your topic with good reasons. They will help you show that your topic makes good sense.

Organizing Your Ideas

Your opinion paragraph should be organized to make it easy for readers to follow what you are trying to tell them. Graphic organizers are a good way to organize your ideas for your writing. The TREE graphic organizer is an effective way to organize your ideas for your opinion paragraphs.

SECTION

Forms of
Writing

T	Topic Sentence	
	Tell what you believe.	
R	Reasons—3 or more	
	Why do I believe this? Will my readers believe this?	
E	Explanations	
	Say more about each reason.	
E	Ending	
	Wrap it up right.	

EXAMPLE Jasmine wants to write an opinion paragraph about the value of playing board games in class. Here is her TREE graphic organizer with her ideas.

T	**Topic Sentence** I think we should be able to play board games in class.
R	**Reason** something different to do in class
E	**Explanation** hard to sit in one place all day
R	**Reason** learn to play fair and take turns
E	**Explanation** teaches kids to get along
R	**Reason** practice math, reading, and spelling
E	**Explanation** fun way to learn
E	**Ending** Board games would help students learn.

After finishing her TREE graphic organizer, Jasmine decided that "practice math, reading, and spelling" is the most important reason to support her opinion. She will save that reason for last in her paragraph.

EXAMPLE Jasmine thought about who would be interested in board games in class. She thought that kids and teachers would be, and maybe parents and the principal, too. Jasmine was sure that if people read her paragraph and agreed with her, there could be board games in class. Here is the opinion paragraph Jasmine wrote. Did she give good reasons to support her opinion?

I think we should be able to play board games in class. One reason why we should play board games is because it would give us something different to do in class. Board games would give kids a break from sitting in one place all day. Since board games teach kids how to play fair and take turns, playing board games would help kids learn to get along. Finally, we should play board games because it would give us practice with math, reading, and spelling. Not only would we be having fun, but we would be learning also.

Try It!

What is Jasmine's opinion about board games? How many reasons does Jasmine give in her paragraph? What linking words does Jasmine use to connect her reasons to her opinion?

Tips for Writing an Opinion Paragraph

STEP 1 Prewriting

▷ What are some things you feel strongly about?
▷ Make a list.
▷ List some reasons to support your opinion.
▷ Put your ideas into a TREE graphic organizer or other web.

SECTION

2

Forms of Writing

STEP 2 Drafting

▷ Use your web to help you remember your reasons.

STEP 3 Revising

▷ **Ideas** Do you have good reasons to support your topic?
▷ **Organization** Did you write your opinion in the first sentence?
▷ **Sentence Fluency** Did you use linking words to connect your opinion and reasons?

STEP 4 Editing/Proofreading

▷ **Conventions** Correct any spelling mistakes.
▷ Does every sentence have an end mark?

STEP 5 Publishing

▷ **Presentation** Write or type a neat final copy.
▷ Draw a picture to go with your paragraph.

Persuasive Letter

Opinion writing can let readers know what you think about something. It can also try to persuade, or make, readers do something. Types of persuasive writing can include persuasive letters, advertising, and even cereal boxes.

Many people write persuasive letters to ask for something. Someday you might write a persuasive letter, too. Maybe your new remote-control robot stops working. You ask the company to send you a new one. Maybe you want information about a recycling project. You think that your school might try this project.

Both of these letters are persuasive. You are asking someone to do something for you. Your letter must give the reader a good reason for doing it. If you ask for a new robot, send a copy of the sales slip from the store. It will show that your robot is brand new. If you ask for information, tell how it will help you or others.

Your persuasive letter should have six parts. You can see them in the letter on the next page. They include the date, inside address, greeting, and body. Your letter should end with a closing and your signature.

As you write, choose your words carefully. You are writing to a busy person—an adult you do not know. Be friendly but polite. Keep your letter short to save your reader time. Do not forget to thank him or her for helping you.

Date ▶   June 14, 2014

Inside ▶   Great Games
Address   11456 Vista Drive
                                    Inglewood, CA 90307

Greeting ▶ Dear Customer Service Department:

Body ▶   I received your new DVD "Kelvin and
Hannah" for my birthday last week. The first
time I tried to watch it, my DVD player said
the disk was unreadable. I am so disappointed.
I wanted to watch it with my friends.

    Would you please send me another copy of
"Kelvin and Hannah"? Here is my address: 1414
Clearview Drive, Oxnard, California 93032. I
want to tell my friends what good service you
have. Then they will buy DVDs from you, too.
Thank you very much for helping me!

Closing ▶   Sincerely,

Signature ▶   Jamal Harrison

SECTION

2

Forms of
Writing

Cereal Box Design

Have you ever taken a good long look at a cereal box? Somebody spent a lot of time and effort designing a cereal box. Why? So you will want that box of cereal. Persuasive writing is not just for the classroom; it's on cereal boxes too!

Ways to Persuade People to Buy

Giving good reasons and facts is one way to get people to buy something. Putting reasons into short phrases that stick in the mind helps people remember them. Describing a thing as the best is another way to persuade people to buy.

EXAMPLE Here is a cereal box designed for people who like healthful foods. It uses reasons and facts to persuade people to try this new "good for you" cereal.

NEW!
Packed with Protein Power!

POWER HOUSE
CEREAL

10 grams of **protein** in every serving
Power Bits of **5** Different Toasted **Whole Grains!**
Iron-Rich Raisins and **Protein**-Rich Sunflower Seeds

Another Look at Cereal Box Design

Here is a cereal box designed for people who like to eat food that looks fun and tastes good. It uses descriptions to persuade people to try this new "fun" cereal.

Try It!

Read the two cereal boxes. Which cereal would you choose? Name three reasons that made you want that cereal.

Poetry

Poetry is very different from other kinds of writing. Think of some poems you have read. They look very different from stories or articles. There is something else about poetry. It can describe things in a way that you may never have thought about before. The lessons on the following pages will give you a chance to write some different kinds of poetry.

Examples of poetry include the following:

▶ Rhyming Poetry
▶ Nonrhyming Poetry
▶ Pattern Poetry

EXAMPLE Lee wrote a poem about his dog.

> There was a little dog named Star
>
> Who liked to run all day.
>
> But oftentimes he'd run too far
>
> And then he'd lose his way.

Continue reading to see more examples and to find out more information about poetry.

Rhyming Poetry

In **poetry** the sound and meaning of words are combined to create images and feelings. Unlike other kinds of writing, poetry is written in lines instead of paragraphs and doesn't always use complete sentences or punctuation. Some poetry rhymes. Three kinds of **rhyming poetry** are the *couplet, triplet,* and *quatrain.*

EXAMPLE

Couplet: Two lines of rhyming poetry.

> I have a friend named Sunny.
>
> She makes me laugh. She's funny!

Triplet: Three lines of rhyming poetry. Rhymes can end every line.

> My balloon sailed up in the sky.
>
> It made me say, "Oh my!"
>
> Then it began to fly.

Quatrain: Four lines of rhyming poetry.

> My silly dog bayed at the moon
> because it had come up too soon.
> He barked, begged, and paced
> but got tired and gave up the chase.

Limerick

Another type of rhyming poem is the **limerick.** Limericks are a special kind of rhyming poetry. Every limerick has five lines. The first, second, and fifth lines rhyme with each other. The third and fourth lines have a different rhyme. Limericks are humorous, or funny, poems.

EXAMPLE Count the syllables as you say each line. Notice that the third and fourth lines each have fewer syllables than the other lines.

> I wish that my room had a floor!
> I don't so much care for a door,
> But this crawling around
> Without touching the ground
> Is getting to be quite a bore!
> —by Gelett Burgess

> There was an old woman from Dover,
> Who ran through a field of blue clover;
> Some very large bees,
> Stung her toes and her knees,
> So, very soon she went back to Dover.

Make a List of Fun Rhyming Words

Before you start to write your poem, make lists of words that rhyme. Make a separate list for each set of rhyming words. Look at the rhyming words lists below. Notice that the ends of the words rhyme even if they are spelled differently.

Rhyming Word List

bee	hatch	maze
flea	catch	days
sea	latch	haze
tea	match	pays
me	scratch	glaze

Reading Your Writing

Poetry is a way for you to share your feelings with your reader. Four rhyming poems are the couplet, the triplet, the quatrain, and the limerick.

Tips for Writing a Rhyming Poem

STEP 1 Prewriting

▷ Read a lot of rhyming poems before you begin.
▷ Pick a subject that is important or funny to you.
▷ List rhyming words to end your lines.
▷ Choose a type of poem: couplet, triplet, quatrain, or limerick.

SECTION

2

Forms of
Writing

STEP 2 Drafting

▷ Write your poem. Use your list of rhyming words.

STEP 3 Revising

▷ **Organization** Do your lines end with rhyming words?
▷ **Sentence Fluency** Lines don't have to be complete sentences, but they do need to sound smooth.

STEP 4 Editing/Proofreading

▷ **Conventions** Correct any spelling mistakes.

STEP 5 Publishing

▷ **Presentation** Make a neat final copy of your poem. You may want to draw a picture to go with it.
▷ Read it aloud to get ready to share it.

Nonrhyming Poetry

Nonrhyming poetry doesn't have rhyming patterns, but it may have other kinds of patterns. For example, *cinquain poems* always have the same kinds of words and number of words. *Free verse* has no patterns at all.

EXAMPLE

Cinquain: A poem that is five lines long and follows this special pattern.

Type of Word	Number of words	
Title	one	"Phone"
Description	two	Quiet, sudden
Action	three	Jingling, jangling, wrangling
Feeling or Effect	four	Demanding I pay attention
Synonym for Title	one	TELEPHONE!!!

Free Verse: A poem that can be long or short. It can have some rhyming words but doesn't have to. Here is a free-verse Crow Indian poem.

"The Sun Is a Yellow-Tipped Porcupine . . ."
The sun is a yellow-tipped porcupine
Lolloping through the sky,
Nibbling treetops and grasses and weeds,
Floating on rivers and ponds,
Casting shining barbed quills at the Earth.

Tips for Writing Free Verse

STEP 1 Prewriting

▷ Make a web with your subject in the middle. Put feelings and thoughts about your subject all around.

STEP 2 Drafting

▷ Write your poem using your web to remember things you want to say.

STEP 3 Revising

▷ **Organization** Read your poem out loud. Every time you pause, begin a new line.

STEP 4 Editing/Proofreading

▷ **Conventions** Make sure your punctuation marks are helping you say what you want.

STEP 5 Publishing

▷ **Presentation** Decide how you want the lines of your free verse to look on the page.
▷ Make a neat final copy.

SECTION

2

Forms of Writing

Reading Your Writing

Poetry is a way for you to share your feelings with your reader. Nonrhyming poetry can have other patterns, but doesn't rhyme.

Pattern Poetry

Some poetry follows rhyming **patterns.** Other poems follow patterns for length of lines. Some poems follow both patterns.

Some poems use the patterns from a familiar poem or song. The words are different, but the rhyme and length of line patterns are the same.

EXAMPLE Do you know the song "I've Been Working on the Railroad"? The poem below uses the same rhyme and line-length patterns.

"We've Been Working on the Tree House"
We've been working on the tree house,
All the weekend long,
We've been sweating and been hammering,
And still it looks all wrong.
Dad, please, please, you have to help us,
Then the job should go fast;
We'll wash the car for you, we promise!
And the tree house will be done at last.

Try It!

Match the familiar song lines to the lines with the same pattern of syllables.

"Happy Birthday to You"
"Yankee Doodle Went to Town"
Will you trade lunch with me
Ever wonder what dogs think

Checklist

▷ Choose a song or poem you know well.
▷ Count the syllables in each line.
▷ List rhyming words that fit your subject.
▷ Sing your song or say your poem out loud as you write. This will help you choose the best words.

Reading Your Writing

Poetry is a way for you to share your feelings with your reader. Some poems can be patterned on other familiar poems or songs.

FUN fact

What is the most familiar song in the English language? "Happy Birthday to You" is the song sung most often. It was written in 1893 by Mildred Hill and Patty Smith Hill.

Timed Writing

Many times in class or for a test, you will have to write a paper in a certain amount of time. For some tests, you may be asked to write a story. For others, you may be asked to write about a topic. For each Timed Writing test you will be given a prompt, directions, and a few reminders that tell you what to write about. Underlining parts of the directions will help you understand the assignment. Making notes about your subject will help you organize your ideas and plan your writing. The following pages will give you additional strategies to help you prepare for Timed Writing tests and tasks.

Examples of timed writing include the following:

- Narrative
- Informative
- Summary
- Response to Literature
- Quick Write

SECTION

2

Forms of
Writing

Narrative

On some tests, the instructions will ask you to write a **narrative.** Narrative writing tells a story. Your story can be true or make-believe but you must be sure to follow the Timed Writing instructions. In your story, you need to tell readers what happened. Your story must have a beginning, a middle, and an end. All good narratives need a setting, a plot, and characters.

Timed Writing Strategies

These strategies will help you when you have a Timed Writing test.

1. Read the entire prompt *twice*. Circle the directions for writing the paper, and underline each thing you are asked to write about. Read through each reminder.
2. Take a few minutes and make notes on what you will write. Make notes for each item you need to write about.
3. Write your paper.
4. Check—Did I respond to each reminder?
5. Revise as needed.

Reminders for Narrative Writing

Here are reminders to use for writing a narrative.

▶ Make sure that each sentence you write helps the reader understand your composition.
▶ Write about your ideas in detail so that the reader understands what you are saying.
▶ Try to use correct spelling, capitalization, punctuation, grammar, and sentences.

On a Timed Writing test, Anna wrote this narrative about going on vacation.

Last summer my mom and dad let my brother and me choose where to go for vacation. They told us we could go to the ocean or to a lake. We chose the ocean, because we had never been there.

We started our trip in the afternoon. My dad drove all night. I don't remember that part though, because I was sleeping. When I woke up, we were just getting there. We could see the ocean in front of us. It was so big, it was almost scary.

We played at the beach every day. We jumped over little waves. We wrote our names in the sand, and we built sand cities.

I felt sad when we had to go home. I took some seashells to help me remember our vacation at the ocean.

Try It!

Should Anna change anything about her writing? Do you think she used the reminders for narrative writing as she wrote her paragraph?

Informative

Informative writing is writing that explains how to do something, or that gives information about something. You may be asked to write an informative paragraph for a Timed Writing test. There are different kinds of informative writing. Book reviews, research reports, and directions are three kinds of informative writing.

SECTION

2

Forms of Writing

Timed Writing Strategies

Follow the strategies below when you have a Timed Writing test.

1. Read the entire prompt *twice*. Circle the directions for writing the paper, and underline each thing you are asked to write about. Read through each reminder.
2. Take a few minutes and make notes on what you will write. Make notes for each item you need to write about.
3. Write your paper.
4. Check—Did I respond to each reminder?
5. Revise as needed.

Reminders for Informative Writing

Use these reminders when you do informative writing.

▶ Stay on topic.
▶ Make sure that each sentence you write helps the reader understand your writing.
▶ Write about your ideas in detail so the reader understands what you are saying.
▶ Try to use correct spelling, capitalization, punctuation, grammar, and sentences.

On a Timed Writing test, Cisco was asked to write a book review of a book he read.

The main characters in <u>Owen Foote, Mighty Scientist</u> are Owen and his best friend, Joseph. They are different from each other in some ways. Owen loves science so much that it is hard for him to see that Joseph doesn't like science very much.

The boys work together on a science fair project with tadpoles. Joseph is afraid that some of the tadpoles are going to die. So he sneaks the tadpoles some extra food. Owen finds the tadpoles dead, and he almost quits the science fair. Then he and Joseph decide to show how things can go wrong in an experiment. They even win a prize for their project.

In the end, Owen understands that Joseph likes other things besides science. But Owen knows they can still be best friends.

Summary

A **summary** is a short way to explain what you have learned from reading. You might take a Timed Writing test that "asks you to read something" and then to write a summary about it. A summary should include the main idea and the other important ideas of what you read.

SECTION 2

Forms of Writing

Writing on Demand Strategies

Use these strategies when you have a Timed Writing test.

1. Read the entire prompt *twice*. Circle the directions for writing the paper, and underline each thing you are asked to write about. Read through each reminder.
2. Take a few minutes and make notes on what you will write. Make notes for each item you need to write about.
3. Write your paper.
4. Check—Did I respond to each reminder?
5. Revise as needed.

Reminders for Writing a Summary

Here are reminders to use when you write a summary.

▶ Choose a text, and write a summary.
▶ Make sure that you include the main ideas.
▶ Make sure that you include the important details.
▶ Try to use correct spelling, capitalization, punctuation, grammar, and sentences.

Grace read a newspaper article about a deer. Then, for her Timed Writing test, she had to write a summary. Here is Grace's summary.

> In October, a deer got its head stuck in a hollow pumpkin. People were afraid it would starve, because the deer could not eat. They tried to help, but the deer ran from them. Then two boys found the broken pumpkin on the ground. Everyone knew the deer was okay.

SECTION

2

Forms of Writing

Try It!

Suppose you had to summarize a news story about a cat. The cat woke a family when there was a fire in the house. Which of these sentences should not be in the summary?

The cat jumped on top of the father and meowed loudly.
The cat had soft gray and white fur.
Everybody ran out of the house and was safe.
The house was filled with smoke.

Response to Literature

Some tests ask you to read a story and respond to it. A response to a story is not a summary of it. Your response should include your own ideas about the story. For example, you might be asked whether you would tell your friends to read it. If so, how would you get them interested in it? Another prompt might ask what you learned from the story.

SECTION

2

Forms of
Writing

Timed Writing Strategies

Use these strategies when you have a Timed Writing test.

1. Read the entire prompt *twice.* Circle the directions for writing the paper, and underline each thing you are asked to write about. Read through each reminder.
2. Take a few minutes to make notes on what you will write. Make notes for each item you need to write about.
3. Write your paper.
4. Check—Did I respond to each reminder?
5. Revise as needed.

Reminders for Responding to Literature

These reminders can help you respond to a story.

▶ Tell what you did and did not like about the story. You might also respond to a character, the setting, or the plot.
▶ Make sure that your sentences are clear and answer the questions in the prompt.
▶ Include details and examples to make your ideas clear.
▶ Check your spelling, capitalization, punctuation, grammar, and sentences.

On a Timed Writing test, Wayne was asked to read a fable called "The Ant and the Grasshopper." Then the prompt told him to do two things:

1. Think of a different title for the story. Explain why your new title fits the story.
2. Explain whether you would change the ending of the story. If so, how?

EXAMPLE Now read how Wayne responded to this prompt.

> I read "The Ant and the Grasshopper" in second grade, too, and I like this story. It shows what can happen if you play all day and do not plan ahead.
>
> 1. I think this story could be called "Some Things Never Change." The story is about talking animals. Yet it could be about people who lived long ago—or today. People—and talking animals—have to learn to take care of themselves. That's how you can tell if someone is grown up. Even today, some people think others should take care of them. Some things never change.
>
> 2. I would change the end of the story and have the ant give the grasshopper some food. It was mean of the ant to let him go hungry. Maybe the grasshopper could have worked to earn the food. He could have cleaned out the anthill!

Quick Write

A quick write is a short, timed writing exercise in which you practice for longer timed writing tests. You will have five to fifteen minutes to plan and write your response to a prompt. The quick write can help you generate ideas for prewriting, writing a summary, or organizing your thoughts. The following are examples of prompts for a quick write practice:

Forms of
Writing

- ▶ Tell the main idea and five facts from the selection.
- ▶ Retell what has happened in the story up to this point.
- ▶ Tell why you agree or disagree with the author.
- ▶ Explain the theme of the story in your own words.

Write Quickly, and Do Not Stop

The goal of a quick write is to express yourself very quickly. Write whatever thoughts you have about the prompt. As long as you continue to write, one idea can lead to the next. Begin writing as soon as possible and continue until your response is complete.

Think of a quick write as a first draft. Do not focus too much on whether you are making mistakes. However, it is important to use correct grammar, spelling, and punctuation. If you still have time remaining after you have finished writing a response, you can edit your work.

Testing Connection

During a quick write, you can practice using the timed writing strategies starting on page 222. Make sure you have included enough information. Even though quick writes are not supposed to be perfectly organized or revised, they will still help you develop skills you need. You can build your confidence in writing a timed response that is focused and logical.

SECTION

2

Forms of Writing

EXAMPLE Marco wrote a quick write on the following prompt: What role does energy have in our daily lives?

> I think energy can be helpful, but it can also be dangerous. People use energy every day. Electricity is energy. My alarm clock needs electricity to work. I have to plug in my computer before I can use it. Gasoline and oil are forms of energy. Our bus needs gas to run. Kids couldn't get to school without energy. My mom and dad need gas and oil to take their cars to work.
>
> Energy can be dangerous, too. Some kinds of energy pollute the air. Also, we need to find new forms of energy to use before our energy runs out. There are other forms of energy that are dangerous too, like lightning and tornadoes. A few weeks ago, lightning hit the power lines, and we lost power. Living without electricity was hard. It made me glad for certain kinds of energy.

Writing Strategies

People read what you write. You want them to enjoy your letters, stories, and poems. You want them to learn from your reports and descriptions. You can help them. Here are some ways to make your writing better.

Ideas

Good writing starts with good ideas. There are lots of ways to get good ideas. You might brainstorm a list of ideas. You might read books or look at pictures. You might make drawings.

Your writing should have a main idea that makes your message clear. Use other ideas to explain or describe the main idea. These other ideas are often called details.

Examples of ideas that can make your writing clearer and more interesting include the following:

▶ Using Drawings
▶ Taking Notes
▶ Combining Ideas
▶ Adding Details
▶ Using Dialogue

Try It!

Suppose you have to write about what a car might look like in 50 years. Brainstorm a drawing to help you get ideas.

Continue reading to see more examples and to find out more information about ideas for your writing.

SECTION
3

Writing Strategies

Using Drawings

You do not always have to use words when you brainstorm. You can use drawings instead. **Drawing** is a great way to get ideas. When you draw, make simple sketches.

You may want to use a drawing when you want to give directions to a place. You might picture a map in your head and then draw the map. You could look at your map to get ideas about what to tell or write. For example, Jose has to give directions that tell how to get from his home to school.

EXAMPLE

School

How would you give directions from your house to your school?

You can also make drawings to help you explain how something happens. What if you want to explain how a seed grows into a tree? You might sketch a seed, then a tiny plant, then a young tree, and then a full-grown tree. Now you can use your drawings to get ideas about what to say. Drawings are also great ways to help you describe imaginary things.

EXAMPLE

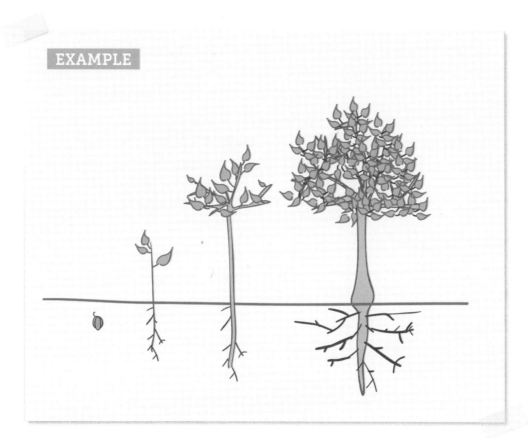

Writing Strategies

Try It!

Draw a picture in your journal of something you would like to write about. Look at your picture later today or tomorrow, and write about it. Was the picture helpful to you? How?

Taking Notes

Taking notes is an important part of writing. To write a report, you need to do research to find factual information. To remember the information, you need to take notes.

When you take notes, you summarize what you read. This is the same whether you are reading a book, a magazine article, a newspaper story, or information on the Internet. Whatever source you use, read the information carefully. Look for important ideas. Look for facts. You will probably have to read the information twice to decide what is most important.

Write your notes on note cards. Write each idea or each fact on a separate card. Try to use just a few words to summarize an idea or a fact. Be sure to use your own words.

EXAMPLE

Lilli is writing a report on the blue whale. Here is one of her note cards.

From <u>Blue Whales Are Big!</u>

Blue whales are the largest whales.

On each card, write down the title of the book or other source you are using, so later you can remember where you got your information.

As you write, remember to write neatly and clearly. You will be very glad you did this when you read your notes later!

Once you have taken all your notes, think about writing your first draft. Read your index cards. Decide which ideas and facts go together.

Make one pile of cards for each paragraph. Probably you will have to change the order of the cards several times before you are ready to write. Use your notes, pile by pile, to help you as you write your report.

Try It!

Read this paragraph. What notes would you take?

Blue whales are huge. Some are as long as 100 feet and can weigh up to about 150 tons. The blue whale is possibly the largest animal on Earth.

SECTION

3

Writing Strategies

Combining Ideas

Combining ideas is a way of revising. After you have written your draft and you are ready to revise, keep the most important ideas and details and take out the details that you do not need.

How do you know what ideas to combine? How do you know what details to take out?

In each paragraph of your writing look for:

▶ short sentences. Can you combine two sentences into one sentence?

▶ sentences with similar ideas. Can you combine these ideas?

▶ details that describe or explain ideas. Can you combine some of the details?

▶ details that do not describe or explain ideas. Cross them out.

▶ details that are repeated. Cross them out.

SECTION

3

Writing
Strategies

Hondo is writing a report about penguins. Here is a paragraph from his first draft. Hondo read the paragraph and crossed out a sentence that had similar ideas to another sentence.

The first time I ever saw a penguin was at the zoo. ~~I liked them a lot.~~ I liked them so much I decided to find out more about them.

Here is another section of Hondo's draft.

Penguins are not like other birds. Penguins do not fly. Penguins are good swimmers. Penguins have flippers. They do not have wings.

Hondo revised the paragraph by combining ideas. Here is how he changed it.

Penguins are not like other birds. Penguins cannot fly because they do not have wings. Instead of wings, they have flippers for swimming. They are very good swimmers.

SECTION

3

Writing Strategies

Try It!

Here is a paragraph from Hondo's draft. How would you tell him to revise it?

Penguins have short feathers. Their feathers are thick. Some of their feathers are white. Some of their feathers are black.

Adding Detail

Good writers revise their drafts to make their writing better. Adding detail is a great way to improve your writing. Details make your writing more interesting to read and make your message clearer.

There are different ways you can add details.

Add an example. Suppose you are describing a tree. In your draft, you wrote, "It is a big tree." Now you are revising your draft. You could show how big the tree is by using a comparison. You might say, "The tree is as tall as the school."

Add facts. You could add facts about the tree. You might say it is 50 years old—even older than the school. You might say that a robin makes its nest in the tree every year.

Add words and phrases that paint a picture. Close your eyes and think about the tree. How could you describe it to someone who never saw it?

Ray wrote a report about the library in his town. Here is part of his draft.

The library is one of my favorite places. They just added a new room. The room is for children. It is one big room! The library is fun. There is a fish tank with goldfish.

Ray revised his draft this way.

The library is one of my favorite places. They just built a new room for children. The room is as big as two classrooms put together!

The library is fun. They have a big fish bowl with a goldfish. The book The Cat in the Hat is right next to it. The first time my friends and I saw it, we laughed out loud because we thought of the goldfish in the book.

Try It!

What details did Ray add to help you know what the library looks like?

Using Dialogue

Dialogue is two or more people talking to each other in a story. Characters seem real when their own words show how they think and feel. Dialogue can also help the action of the story move along quickly.

Writers use quotation marks to show the words that the characters speak. When you use quotation marks, readers will know someone is speaking.

EXAMPLE

In "The Country Mouse and the City Mouse," Vidas Barzdukas uses dialogue to move the story along and to show the characters' thoughts and feelings.

Country Mouse gave her cousin a tour of the farm. They visited green pastures and a pond surrounded by purple and yellow lilacs. City Mouse sat down on a rock and smiled contentedly.

"It sure is quiet and peaceful here," City Mouse remarked. "What do you do for excitement?"

"I do lots of things!" Country Mouse answered. "I watch the clouds and listen to the birds sing. I count the number of croaks from the bullfrogs in the pond. Sometimes I collect colorful leaves all day long!"

"That doesn't sound too exciting to me," City Mouse mumbled to herself.

Look at the example of dialogue you just read. Notice the paragraph indent. This was a signal that a character began to speak. That makes it easier for the reader to tell who is talking. Speaker tags, a group of words beginning with a person's name and a word like *said*, *asked*, or *answered*, help too.

Try It!

Match the dialogue quote with the speaker tag.

▶ "You can play basketball in a wheelchair?"

▶ "Just watch me!"

▶ Jason answered as he stole the ball and sped off.

▶ Nancy asked as she caught the ball.

Reading Your Writing

Dialogue can add interest to your story and help make your characters seem real. You can also tell part of the story through dialogue.

Organization

You can have the best ideas in the world for a story or a report. But if you do not organize those ideas, your readers will not understand what you mean.

Organizing begins with prewriting. Good writers plan what they will write. Good writing must have a beginning, a middle, and an end.

Organizing is also part of the revising process. Good writers check to see that their ideas are in an order that makes the best sense.

Examples of ways to organize your writing include the following:

- ▶ Graphic Organizers
- ▶ Story Elements
- ▶ Using an Outline
- ▶ Sequence

Try It!

Here are three facts. Continue reading to find out how to put them in an outline.

Found underground

Diamonds

Used to make jewlery

Graphic Organizers

A graphic organizer can be a useful tool for writers. You can use it during prewriting to gather your ideas and put them in order. There are many kinds of graphic organizers. Choose one that works with the type of writing you are doing, or create one of your own.

Story Map

This one is useful when you plan to write a story.

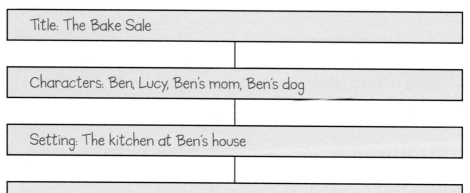

Title: The Bake Sale

Characters: Ben, Lucy, Ben's mom, Ben's dog

Setting: The kitchen at Ben's house

Plot (What Happened)

Beginning (Problem): Ben and Lucy are supposed to bring three dozen cookies for a bake sale at their school.

Middle (Events):
1. Ben's mom helps him and Lucy bake the cookies.
2. Ben and Lucy let the cookies cool before icing them.
3. Ben and Lucy come back and see that Ben's dog has eaten all of the cookies.

Ending (How the problem was solved):
Ben and Lucy use their allowance money to buy cookies for the school bake sale.

Venn Diagram

This graphic organizer is useful when you are comparing and contrasting two things. It is called a **Venn diagram.**

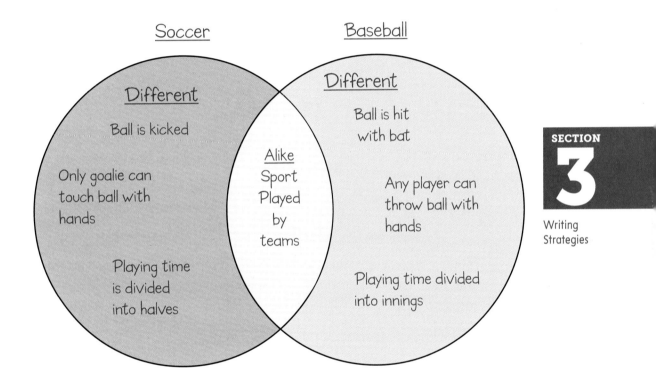

Soccer

Baseball

Different

Ball is kicked

Only goalie can touch ball with hands

Playing time is divided into halves

Alike
Sport
Played
by
teams

Different

Ball is hit with bat

Any player can throw ball with hands

Playing time divided into innings

SECTION

3

Writing Strategies

Webs

Some graphic organizers help you gather ideas to describe something.

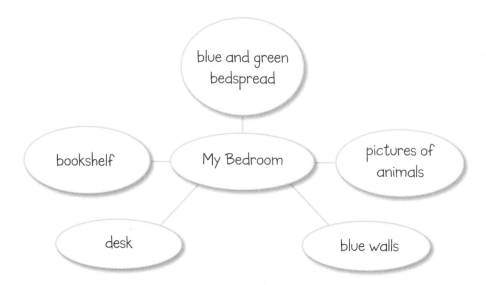

Reading Your Writing

Graphic organizers help you make a plan for your writing. Taking the time to collect and organize your ideas will make what you write easier to read.

TREE Graphic Organizer

Some graphic organizers help you organize your ideas for an opinion paragraph.

T	Topic Sentence Tell what you believe.	
R	Reasons—3 or more Why do I believe this? Will my readers believe this?	
E	Explanations Say more about each reason.	
E	Ending Wrap it up right.	

Try It!

Which graphic organizer would you use for planning to write about each of the ideas below?

▶ describe a puppy

▶ write a story

▶ show how lions and tigers are alike and different

▶ write your opinion about school recess

Story Elements

There are many times you will be asked to write a narrative. Narrative writing tells a story, and a story needs characters and a setting. Some kinds of narrative writing also need a plot.

You can organize your story using a graphic organizer such as a chart. Write the words *Characters*, *Setting*, and *Plot* on the chart. Your chart might look like this:

Characters	Setting	Plot

When you begin your story, you may already have an idea for the plot. In that case, write your idea down in the Plot column. Fill in as much of the chart as you can. As you think about the characters, setting, and plot, add ideas and make changes.

If you cannot think of an idea, try brainstorming. Start to brainstorm on plot, characters, or setting.

Suppose you decide to start with the setting. Ask yourself:

▶ "Who would live in this setting?"

▶ "What would happen in this setting?"

Suppose you decide to start with the characters. Ask yourself:

▶ "Where would these characters live?"

▶ "What would these characters do?"

Suppose you decide to start with the plot. Ask yourself:

▶ "Which characters would be part of the plot?"

▶ "Where would the story take place?"

SECTION

3

Writing
Strategies

Each decision will lead to more ideas for your story.

Try It!

Grant is writing a story. He picks the zoo for his setting, but he cannot think of what else to write. Help Grant out by giving him ideas for a plot and characters.

Using an Outline

Suppose you are going to write a report, a book review, or a news story. You have already taken notes to get the information you need. Now you need to organize your notes so you can write your draft. An **outline** is a useful way to organize ideas and information.

An outline helps you sort out the most important information and the details. It also helps you decide where the information goes. An outline helps you answer these questions:

> ▸ What are the most important points?
>
> ▸ What are the most important details?
>
> ▸ Which information should go at the beginning of your draft?
>
> ▸ Which information should go in the middle?
>
> ▸ Which information should go at the end?

An outline is a written plan that follows a pattern. In an outline, there is a place to put each main idea. There are also places to put the details that support each main idea. An outline uses roman numerals, capital letters, numbers, and lowercase letters to show how important each idea is.

EXAMPLE Sylvie is writing a book review. She has used her notes to make this outline. Notice that she starts with the title and author of her book. Then she begins her outline.

SECTION
3

Writing
Strategies

Betsy-Tacy
By Maud Hart Lovelace
I. Two best friends
   A. Betsy
      1. True story
      2. Maud Hart Lovelace is Betsy
   B. Tacy
      1. Moves into house across from Betsy
      2. Becomes friend at birthday party
II. Three best friends
   A. Betsy and Tacy leave calling card
   B. Tib's mother visits Mrs. Ray
   C. Girls meet Tib

When Sylvie finishes her outline, she will read it over. She will probably make some changes and then start her draft.

Sequence

Sequence is the order in which things happen. The sequence of events tells you what comes first and what happens after that.

Sequence is a very important way to organize your writing. Sometimes a sequence will describe a process like cooking. When you give directions you use sequence too.

As a good writer you know the sequence of events or ideas for each piece of your writing. You need to make sure that the sequence of events or ideas makes sense to your readers.

Try It!

Put the following sentences in the correct order.

I went swimming.

I rode my bike to the pool.

I woke up.

I put on sunscreen.

SECTION

3

Writing
Strategies

As you revise your writing, you can add certain words to help your readers understand the sequence. Here are some of the words you can use.

first	second	third
finally	next	then
later	before	after

EXAMPLE Jennifer is revising a report about frogs. Below are two paragraphs from her report. Notice the words she added that help show the sequence.

first
The big change is when the eggs turn into

tadpoles. These tadpoles look a lot like fish. Next

The tadpoles grow back legs. The legs are

called hind legs.   Soon

The tadpoles grow front legs. The tadpoles

look like tiny frogs, but they still have little tails.

Their lungs are growing so they will be able to

At last,
breathe air. The frogs grow bigger, and their tails

disappear. They are ready to live on the land.

Research

Research involves using sources to find information on a topic. Good researchers use many sources when investigating. As a researcher, you must decide which resources will be most helpful for you. Use encyclopedias, atlases, books, magazines, interviews, newspapers, journals, films, and the Internet.

You will use technology and other sources as you research information. Different sources can include the following:

- ▶ Nonfiction Books
- ▶ Encyclopedias
- ▶ Dictionaries
- ▶ Magazine Articles
- ▶ Newspaper Articles
- ▶ Interviews
- ▶ Maps
- ▶ Internet Web Sites

Try It!

Suppose you want to write a report on whales. Which sources could you use to research information for your report?

SECTION

3

Writing Strategies

Continue reading this section of the Handbook to find out information about researching information.

Research and Technology

Luis has been asked to write about earthquakes. He does not know much about them. How should he start?

Luis cannot explain everything there is to know about earthquakes. That would be a very long report! Instead, he should think of a question that interests him. Luis wonders why so many earthquakes take place in California.

Now Luis has a question to answer. Next, he should use what he knows to guess the answer. This guess is called a conjecture. Luis thinks for a while. Maybe California has so many earthquakes because it is on the edge of North America. Now Luis has formulated a conjecture.

Luis's next step is to do research—collect facts. These facts will tell him whether his conjecture is correct. Where can he find facts?

A **dictionary** will tell him the definition of *earthquake*. That's a good start. Like a dictionary, an encyclopedia has topics in alphabetical order. Luis looks under *e* for earthquakes. The **encyclopedia** tells him what causes earthquakes. It explains where they occur. It also tells what kinds of damage they can cause.

Now Luis knows where most earthquakes happen. He uses an **atlas** of maps to find these places.

When Luis finds a map of where earthquakes happen, he smiles. This map helps answer his question! Most earthquakes occur around the edge of the Pacific Ocean. That's where California is. Earth is covered with huge, rocky plates. Several of them meet at the edge of the Pacific. When these plates push against each other, they can cause earthquakes.

Still, Luis knows that he should look in more than one place for facts. His father helps him check the Internet. They use a search engine. It helps you find information.

First, you type a keyword. Luis types *earthquakes*. Then the search engine shows pages and pages of Web sites about earthquakes. It lists more than thirteen million sites!

Luis knows that he can make his search more specific by adding more keywords. He types *where earthquakes happen kids*. The word *kids* will help him find Web sites meant for young people. Now the search engine lists nearly two million sites. Luis can read and understand many of them. He collects more facts about earthquakes.

Now Luis knows that his conjecture is almost correct. California has earthquakes because it is on the edge of the Pacific Ocean, not the edge of North America. The East Coast of North America has very few earthquakes. Yet the West Coast has many earthquakes. It is along the Pacific Ocean.

Luis did research to answer his question. Now he can organize his notes and write his report. He will share what he learned with his classmates. They live in California. They need to know about earthquakes!

SECTION

3

Writing
Strategies

Sources

If you need to write a report, then you will have to do research. Research is fun to do. There are many interesting sources where you can get information.

A **source** can be:

▶ a nonfiction book

▶ an encyclopedia

▶ a dictionary

▶ a magazine article

▶ an interview

▶ an atlas

▶ a CD-ROM

▶ a television program

▶ a newspaper story

▶ information on the Internet

SECTION

3

Writing
Strategies

You will find nonfiction books on just about every topic you can think of. It is a good idea to skim through a book to see if it has the information you need. Read the table of contents in the front of the book. Look at a few pages inside the book.

Encyclopedias have many articles on many different topics. The topics are arranged alphabetically. So, for example, if you want to know about dolphins, you would look for the part that starts with the letter *D*.

Sometimes a source may have information that is wrong. This is especially true for information you find on the Internet. Web sites from history and science museums are good sources. The information on these sites has been checked carefully. Your teacher or librarian can help you find Web sites with correct information.

Be sure to write down the titles of the sources you use. Then if you want to go back to a source, you know which one to look for.

SECTION
3

Writing
Strategies

Try It!

Skim through nonfiction books in your classroom. Read the table of contents. Look at the index at the end of the book to see the different topics. Flip through a few pages to see the pictures. Read a few paragraphs to see if the book is easy to understand.

Vocabulary Strategies

Writers are like builders. Good builders use the best material they can get to build the strongest buildings they can build. Good writers use the best, most precise words to write the best sentences they can. Good, strong sentences make great writing. The more you know about words and how to use them, the better writer you will be.

SECTION

3

Writing
Strategies

Examples of different types of vocabulary words that can be used to enhance your writing include the following:

- ▶ Transition Words
- ▶ Vivid Language
- ▶ Figurative Language
- ▶ Descriptive Words
- ▶ Precise Word Choice
- ▶ Formal Language

Try It!

Read the following words:
- ▶ said
- ▶ cried
- ▶ sad
- ▶ ran

Can you think of examples of better word choices for these words?

Continue reading this section of the Handbook to find out more information about vocabulary strategies.

Transition Words

Suppose you are writing a research report or a book review. You need to find ways to help your readers see how the information fits together. You can do this by adding transition words. **Transition words** are words that help readers understand how the information is connected. Transition words also make your writing sound better.

Some transition words are very simple. You use them when you combine sentences. They include *and, but,* and *because.*

Some transition words show the order in which things happen. Here are some order words.

first	second	last
now	then	next
before	after	finally

Other transition words show the location where things happen. Below are some location words.

above	below	in the middle
left	right	outside
inside	near	far

EXAMPLE Here is part of a research report that Teddy wrote about a mountain. He used his notes to write his first draft.

> Mount Saint Helens is a mountain in Washington. A volcano started to act up in March 1980. There were little earthquakes and explosions. A bulge grew on the mountain. On May 18, 1980, the volcano erupted. It blew part of the mountain away.

Teddy decided to add some transition words and to move some other words around. The changes are underlined so you can see them easily.

SECTION

3

Writing
Strategies

> Mount Saint Helens is a mountain in Washington. In March 1980, a volcano started to act up. At first, there were little earthquakes and explosions. Then a bulge grew on the side of the mountain. On May 18, 1980, the volcano erupted. It blew part of the mountain away.

Vivid Language

When you read a good book, does the story come to life in your mind? Can you picture the characters as they move and talk? Can you hear their voices? When you do that, you are visualizing what is happening. Good writers use **vivid language** to make their writing come alive.

Vivid Language and the Five Senses

The five senses are sight, hearing, smell, taste, and touch. What do they have to do with vivid language? Everything! Vivid language is words and details that make you feel like you are inside a story or an event. Vivid language can help you imagine a big silver moon. Or it can make you feel a tickly, tiny, cold snowflake on your nose. Vivid language can also make you almost hear, smell, and taste things.

SECTION
3

Writing
Strategies

It does not matter if you are writing a fictional story or telling about a real event. Vivid language will make your writing better. You can add vivid language to your writing by following these steps.

▶ Read your draft. Then close your eyes and picture the characters. Now read your draft again. Is there anything you can add to help your readers see or feel what you did?

▶ This time, close your eyes and picture the setting. Read your draft again. What can you add to your writing that will help readers feel as if they were there?

Try It!

Lolita is writing a story. The setting is the woods at midnight. This is what she has written so far.

The moon was shining down on the trees. The wind was blowing.

Think of two things you could add to the sentences to make readers feel more like they are there.

SECTION

3

Writing Strategies

Figurative Language

Good writers use **figurative language** to make their writing more interesting. Figurative language helps readers imagine what something is like.

There are three main kinds of figurative language: simile, metaphor, and personification. By sprinkling a metaphor here and a simile there, you make your writing more fun to read.

Simile

A simile is a way of comparing something using the words *like* or *as*. Here are some examples.

> He swims like a fish.
>
> His sneeze was as loud as thunder.

Often you hear people say the same similes. It is better if you can think of your own.

Try It!

How would you finish each of these similes? (*Use your imagination!*)

The car was as slow as _____.

The house is as tall as _____.

Metaphor

A metaphor is a way of comparing something *without* using the words *like* or *as*. Both the examples below are metaphors.

My brain is jelly.

She is an Einstein when she does math.

In the first example, the writer wanted readers to know that he was confused. His brain was just like jelly! This writer also wanted his readers to laugh at the description. Figurative language can be funny, or sad, or just interesting.

Personification

Personification is a way to talk about an animal or a thing as if it were a person. Notice the word person in *personification*. Suppose you wanted to say that the moon was shining on some trees. If you used personification, you might say it this way.

The moon smiled down on the trees below.

SECTION 3

Writing Strategies

Try It!

What kind of figurative language is used in the sentence below?
The flowers danced in the wind.

Descriptive Words

Words are wonderful! When you choose the right words, you can paint a picture in the minds of your readers. Good writers use action words and describing words in their writing.

Action Words

Action words tell you what someone or something is doing. There are many action words. Three examples are *jump, laughing,* and *ran.* Those are all good action words, but other words might paint a more interesting or clearer picture. For example, suppose you wrote, "Ginger *ran* down the street." Instead of the word *ran,* you might choose *sped, raced,* or *dashed.*

SECTION

3

Writing Strategies

Try It!

Think of another word for *shouted* in the sentence below.
John <u>shouted</u> as loud as he could.

Describing Words

Describing words tell how something looks, feels, smells, sounds, or tastes. Suppose you want to describe how big a dinosaur was. You could use the word *big* or *large.* You could also use *huge, giant-size, gigantic, monster-size, immense,* or *towering.*

Shades of Meaning

Some words mean almost the same thing. Yet they are different enough to give readers very different pictures. Here are two sentences. They are both about laughing. Notice how they are different.

Sarah giggled when she read the book.

Sarah roared with laughter when she read the book.

SECTION

3

Writing
Strategies

Reading Your Writing

When you are revising, look at your action and describing words. The right words help your readers see the picture you want them to see.

Precise Word Choice

When you write, use words that are precise. For example, instead of using the word *bird,* you might use the word for the specific bird, like *robin* or *eagle.* Both these words are more precise than the word *bird,* because they tell you what kind of bird. Precise words make your writing more clear.

When you search for precise words, think like a scientist. Scientists are very good at observing and then telling what they see.

Look at the word *person* in the sentence below.

The person came to our house.

The word *person* does not tell you very much. So think like a scientist. What might you know about the person to tell your readers? Was the person a man? Was the person a neighbor? Was the person old?

SECTION

3

Writing
Strategies

Look at the next sentence.

Aunt Callie made biscuits.

You might change it this way.

Aunt Callie <u>baked</u> <u>buttermilk</u> biscuits.

The words *baked* and *buttermilk* paint a clearer picture for readers.

EXAMPLE There is more than one way to change the same sentence by adding precise words. Look at this sentence.

> The mouse made a noise.

One way to change it is this way.

> The mouse squeaked.

The word *squeaked* is more precise than the words *made a noise.* You could also change it to

> The field mouse made a squeaky noise.

The word *field* tells you what kind of mouse it was. *Squeaky* tells you what kind of noise the mouse made. As you can see, both are good ways to make a change.

Try It!

Change the underlined words to make the sentence more precise.
The visitor <u>said something</u> to our class.

Formal Language

There are different kinds of writing. One kind is formal writing. Formal writing is serious, rather than friendly. Examples of formal writing are research reports and business letters. Another kind of writing is informal writing. A letter to a friend is an example of informal writing. When you do formal writing, it is important to use **formal language.**

Spell Words Out

When you use formal language, you do not use contractions. For example,

Use	Do not use
is not	isn't
you are	you're
cannot	can't

When you use formal language, you do not use abbreviations. For example,

Use	Do not use
television	TV
Mount Rainier	Mt. Rainier
pajamas	PJs

Choose Grown-Up Words

Use words that sound grown-up. For example, suppose you are writing a research report about rabbits. It is better to talk about the *mother rabbit* rather than the *mommy bunny*.

Use Correct Spellings

Correct spelling is an important part of formal language. Sometimes when you write messages to your friends, you might not double-check your spelling. When you use formal language, you need to double-check for correct spelling.

Why is Formal Language Important?

Why is it important to use formal language in formal writing like a research report? When you use formal language, your audience will pay better attention to your message.

SECTION

3

Writing
Strategies

Try It!

In your head, say the following sentence using more formal language.
Hey, Janie, how's your summer vacation goin'?

Voice

Voice is the way you speak through your writing. It is the trait that makes your writing your very own. Voice is what separates your writing from someone else's writing.

To write with a strong voice, you need to know your purpose for writing. Do you want to tell facts about your favorite city? Do you want to explain how to plant flowers? Perhaps you want to write a letter to your best friend. Your voice will change when writing for different purposes.

SECTION

3

Writing
Strategies

You might change your voice for the following reasons:

▶ Audience and Purpose
▶ Creating Mood
▶ Creating Suspense

Try It!

Read the following sentence. Then continue reading this section of the Handbook to find out how to change the voice of this sentence so that it portrays a calm and peaceful mood.

Sarah and her family waited anxiously in the basement for the severe storm to pass.

Audience and Purpose

You can call your cousin on the phone. You can talk to a friend at school. You can write a letter to your grandmother. These are all ways to communicate with another person.

Writing is a special way to communicate because the people you write can save what you write and read it again. You can also plan what you want to say and change it before you send your letter.

The three most important things to think about when you write are **what, why,** and **who.**

1. *What* is the topic you want to write about.
2. *Why* is your **purpose** for writing. You can *entertain, inform, explain,* and *persuade* with writing.
3. *Who* is the **audience** that will read your writing. You can change what you write about and the words you use to fit your audience.

Good writers communicate their thoughts well. They do this by keeping their audience and purpose in mind while they are planning, writing, and changing their writing.

SECTION

3

Writing
Strategies

Types of Writing

The purpose of your writing will help you decide what kind of writing to use. Look at the following purposes and examples of writing.

Entertain
  poem

Inform
  summary

Persuade
  poster

Remember Things
  to-do list

Record Information
  learning log

Keep in Touch
  friendly letter

Try It!

Can you think of other types of writing for each purpose listed above? What are some other writing purposes and types of writing that would help meet these purposes?

SECTION

3

Writing
Strategies

EXAMPLE Danielle likes to make up stories to entertain her four-year-old brother, Marty. She thought of one while he was sleeping. Danielle started to write her story down so she wouldn't forget it.

> Once upon a time, there was a boy named Marty who had a giant bird for a friend. The bird's name was Swifty. He was just the right size to take Marty for rides.
>
> When everyone else was asleep, Swifty would come and take Marty for a ride. Every night they would fly to a different place!
>
> Last night, Swifty and Marty flew to Alaska. They saw whales and polar bears. Then they saw a pirate ship. Marty warned the people in the town. He saved them from the pirates.

The purpose of Danielle's story is to entertain. She likes to tell Marty stories to make him smile.

Danielle knows her audience very well, so she picked a subject that he likes. She knows that Marty likes birds and loves to hear stories about himself. Because Marty is just four years old, Danielle doesn't use big words or long sentences.

EXAMPLE Ryan wanted to tell his grandmother about his winning goal in the soccer game. He decided to write her a letter.

> 1735 Juniper Way
> Boaz, Alabama 35957
> September 8, 2014
>
> Dear Grandma,
>
>   We played our first soccer game on Saturday, and guess what? I got the only goal in the whole game!
>
>   It was almost the end of the game when I finally got the ball. I ran all the way up the field and past all the other players! I made a fake move to the right. When the goalie moved to follow my fake, I kicked and scored!
>
>   You should've been there, Grandma. Everyone was jumping up and down and cheering. I hope you can come see one of my games. If you do, be sure to wear your jumping shoes!
>
> Love,
> Ryan

Ryan's purpose was to inform his grandmother about his winning goal in the soccer game. Ryan's audience was his grandmother. He knew she would like to know about his goal.

EXAMPLE Cortland wanted to write an informative paragraph about the first airplane flight. Because his purpose is to inform, he knew he needed to include several facts and details in his paragraph.

> The First Flight
> On December 17, 1903, Wilbur and Orville Wright flew an airplane in Kitty Hawk, North Carolina. The plane stayed in the air for twelve seconds. The plane flew about 118 feet. The brothers had been trying to fly since 1896.

When you are writing to inform, you are giving information about a subject. It's important to think about your audience. What might your audience already know? What does your audience need to know?

Try It!

Read Cortland's informative paragraph. What facts did Cortland include in his paragraph?

Has the Purpose Been Met?

Understanding your purpose for writing before you start is important. The purpose will focus your ideas and guide your writing. When you go back and read your writing, ask yourself whether your writing does what you wanted it to do. Did you meet the purpose?

EXAMPLE Terrance wants to make people laugh. He wrote a fairy tale. Has his purpose been met?

> Once upon a time, there lived a handsome prince. He was fishing one day when he caught a talking fish! "Put me back in the water now!" the fish said and hit the prince's nose with his tail. The prince was angry and put the fish in a bowl of water. He took the fish back to the castle. As punishment, he made the fish tell him a joke every day.
>
> One day, the fish said, "Knock, Knock."
>
> The prince replied, "Who's there?"
>
> "Canoe," answered the fish.
>
> "Canoe who?" asked the prince.
>
> "Can you please let me go?"
>
> The prince laughed so hard, he decided to set the fish free. Everyone lived happily ever after.

Match each writing purpose and topic with an audience.

Entertain with fishing stories and jokes	Students, Teachers
Persuade to serve tacos once a week	3rd Grade Class
Inform about new books in library	Friend
Explain how to fly a kite	School Officials

Here are three ways thinking about your audience and purpose will help you stay in touch with your readers.

1. **Ideas:** Different ideas and topics will be interesting to different audiences. Be sure to pick a topic that will interest your readers.
2. **Word Choice:** Different words are used when writing for different age groups. Check to make sure your readers are able to understand what you write.
3. **Voice:** Different voices are used for different purposes. Use a friendly voice to entertain and a polite voice to explain.

Reading Your Writing

Take time to decide on your audience and purpose before you begin writing. You will be more successful in communicating with your reader.

Creating Mood

Mood is a feeling that readers get when they are reading a piece of writing. When you write with a strong voice, you create a mood that your readers can feel.

Think of different pictures. Imagine a picture with a blue sky, a shining sun, and baby animals on a farm. That picture creates a happy mood. Now think of a dark, stormy picture. Trees are blowing in the wind, and lightning bolts streak across the sky. That picture creates a very different mood.

Usually, it is not just one thing that creates the mood. In writing, mood is created by the words and the details you choose to include.

Try It!

Change the mood of this sentence to a cheerful mood.
The boy raced out of the big, dark room, dashed down the creaky stairs, and flew out the front door.

SECTION

3

Writing Strategies

Before You Start

First, you need to choose your purpose for writing and know what you are going to write about. You can set the mood in informative writing or narrative writing.

Creating Mood

Ask yourself:

▶ What words can I use to paint a picture in the reader's mind?
▶ What details can I tell my readers that will help them understand my purpose?
▶ What words can I use to describe sounds, smells, and sights?

Try It!

If you were writing a story about a time you visited an old farmhouse what type of mood would you want to create? Would the farmhouse be a scary place or a welcoming place? What words would you use to describe the sounds, smells, and sights of the farmhouse?

EXAMPLE Rick is writing a story for the class newspaper. He is describing the first time he went on a roller coaster. He wants to create a mood that makes his readers feel they are with him. Rick wrote two different beginning paragraphs.

> I get into my seat and buckle my seat belt. The roller coaster begins to climb up a big hill. Maybe I should close my eyes. I hang on tight as we go up the hill.

> I climb into the little car and buckle my seat belt. We are starting to roll forward. Uh-oh, we are speeding up! In a way, I want to close my eyes, but I don't. I grip the bar so tightly my hands feel numb.

Which paragraph creates a better mood? What words does Rick use to create his mood? Can you imagine being on the roller coaster with him?

SECTION

3

Writing
Strategies

Creating Suspense

Stories with suspense are fun to read. They can be fun to write, too! Suspense is an excitement caused by not knowing what is going to happen. Two kinds of suspense stories are mysteries and adventure stories.

Mysteries

A mystery is a type of story in which a crime, puzzle, or mysterious happening is solved or explained by a central character. Suspense is created in a mystery story to keep the readers "guessing" about the outcome of the story. This creates anticipation and keeps the reader reading.

Adventure Stories

An adventure story is an exciting fictional story with characters, places, and events that seem real. Suspense, action, and danger are the important features in adventure stories. These features help keep the story exciting.

> **EXAMPLE** Look at a paragraph from Sarah's adventure tale. Was she able to create suspense? What do you think will happen next?

> Nathan jumped into the car and sped away down the dirt road. The road snaked down into the trees and disappeared. He couldn't see where it went. Nathan stomped on the brakes, but the car didn't stop. Nathan tried to keep the car under control as it raced down the narrow road.

Suspense Strategies

Descriptive Words

When you write a suspense story, describe odd sounds, and use descriptive adjectives to suggest danger or surprise. The action in good suspense writing is clear and exciting. For example, instead of saying someone "was walking around the house," you can say the person "was creeping through the house."

Details

Try to build suspense by giving a few details at a time. Suppose you are writing about a secret tomb. Don't just say that a character found the tomb. Instead, you can build the suspense first. You can say: Henry looked down and saw something gleaming. It was a gold ring. He couldn't believe his eyes!

SECTION

3

Writing
Strategies

Surprise

You might want to add a surprise to your story. A surprise is when something sudden or unexpected happens. You could tell your readers that Henry picked up the ring, fell backward, and landed on the door of the tomb. Surprises make the story exciting and sometimes funny!

Sentence Fluency

Good writing is like good music. It sounds good! What makes it sound good? The answer is sentence fluency.

Sentence fluency means the way you arrange your sentences so that they read smoothly. When your writing reads smoothly, one sentence flows into the next. Smooth writing is easier to read. It is more interesting to read too!

SECTION

3

Writing
Strategies

Elements of sentence fluency include the following:

▶ Sentence Beginnings
▶ Varying Sentences

EXAMPLE Sentences that all begin the same way sound boring! Read this paragraph.

I have a new pair of roller skates. I got them for my birthday. I have always wanted to try roller skates. I use my skates every day.

Continue reading this section of the Handbook to see more examples and to find out more information about sentence fluency.

SECTION

3

Writing
Strategies

Sentence Beginnings

Each sentence in a piece of writing should begin a different way. Read the following paragraph.

> Lin went to the zoo with her aunt. Lin saw lions and elephants at the zoo. Lin liked the elephants best.

As you can see, each sentence begins the same way. You can change the beginning of some of the sentences to make them more interesting.

One way to change the beginning of a sentence is to use a pronoun instead of a noun. For example

> <u>She</u> saw lions and elephants at the zoo.

In the sentence above, the pronoun *she* takes the place of the noun *Lin*.

You can add transition words. You might say

> <u>First</u>, Lin saw the lions. <u>Next</u>, she saw the elephants.

You could also change it this way.

> Lin saw the lions <u>first, and then</u> she saw the elephants.

You can change the order of the words in a sentence. You might say

At the zoo, she saw lions and elephants.

Another way to change the beginning is to change the subject of the sentence. In the sentence below, *elephants* is the subject, not *Lin*.

The elephants are the animals Lin liked best.

Here are some things to remember.

▶ There are many ways to make the beginnings of sentences different.
▶ You do not have to wait until you are revising. As you write your draft, try to make the beginnings of your sentences special.
▶ When you are revising, look at the sentences that are next to each other. See if they begin the same way. Then change one of them.
▶ You do not have to make the beginning of *every* sentence different.

SECTION
3

Writing
Strategies

Varying Sentences

To make your writing as interesting as possible, use different kinds of sentences. Do you remember the four kinds of sentences? They are declarative, interrogative, exclamatory, and imperative.

The *declarative* sentence is the one we use most. It tells something and has a period at the end. Here is an example.

Squirrels usually have gray fur.

Declarative sentences are perfectly good sentences, as you can see. But a whole paragraph full of them can be boring.

What can you do to make your paragraph more interesting? You can add an *interrogative* statement. An interrogative statement is a question and ends in a question mark. Like this:

What color fur does a squirrel have?

SECTION

3

Writing
Strategies

Reading Your Writing

Use different types of sentences when you write. You can use declarative, interrogative, exclamatory, or imperative sentences. Be sure to use the correct end mark.

Try adding an *imperative* sentence. An imperative sentence is a command and ends with a period. It tells you to do something.

Look at that squirrel climbing the tree.

An *exclamatory* sentence shows strong feeling and ends in an exclamation point!

That squirrel has a white head and a brown body!

Try It!

First Daniel wrote:
A little cat was making the noise.
Then he changed it to
What was making the noise? It was a little cat.
How did he change his writing?

Conventions

Just as there are rules for understanding math and for playing games, there are rules for writing. In writing, the rules are called **conventions**. Understanding the rules of math makes learning math easier. It is impossible to play a game without knowing the rules. Without writing conventions, people would have an awful time reading anything. Imagine if there were no capital letters or periods in the sentences in this paragraph. You would not be able to tell where one sentence ended and the next began. You can see why it is important to know about writing conventions.

SECTION

3

Writing
Strategies

Remember to check for the following conventions before presenting a piece of writing:

▶ Penmanship
▶ Proofreading
▶ Evaluating and Revising

Penmanship

Do you write neatly? Many people, including many adults, do not. Messy writing can cause problems. For example, mail carriers cannot read the addresses on some letters. Those letters may end up in the wrong mailbox.

Do you have any of these problems in penmanship?

SECTION

3

Writing
Strategies

▶ The letters in words are too crowded.
Leave space between each letter. Take time to form each letter instead of rushing to write the next one.

▶ The words all run together.
To fix this problem, use two pencils. Write with one of them. Lay the other pencil between words, with the tip pointed away from you. The spaces between your words should be about as wide as that pencil.

▶ The lines of writing are too close together.
Writing on lined paper will help you get used to leaving enough space between lines.

▶ The pages are covered with writing.
Neat writing leaves about an inch of space at both side margins and at the bottom of the page. Plan your writing so you do not use that space.

▶ The letters slant in different directions.
Letters that point in all directions look messy. Practice slanting all of your letters the same.

▶ The letters are different sizes.
Tall letters, such as *l* and *h*, should all be the same height. Letters with tails, such as *g* and *y*, should all be the same length. Similar letters, such as *o* and *a*, should be about the same size.

How should you place your paper? This student is right-handed. The paper is straight in front of the student. The writing hand is below the writing. The other hand is holding the paper. Are you left-handed? Then you might slant the paper slightly to the right. Keep it parallel to your left forearm.

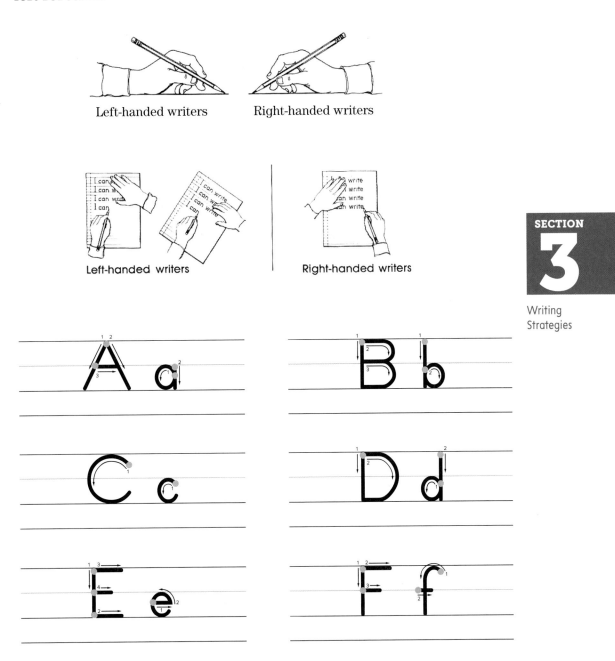

Left-handed writers   Right-handed writers

Left-handed writers   Right-handed writers

A a

B b

C c

D d

E e

F f

Proofreading

Even the best writers need to proofread their work. **Proofreading** means reading to find and fix mistakes. When you proofread, you check to make sure you have followed the conventions of good writing.

The conventions of good writing include:

- spelling words correctly
- using words correctly
- beginning sentences with capital letters
- using capital letters for people's names and the names of places
- ending sentences with the correct punctuation
- indenting paragraphs
- writing clear, effective sentences

It is very easy to make mistakes when you write. You might forget to add a word. Or you might spell something wrong. Perhaps you forgot to put a period at the end of a sentence. You can use proofreading marks when you edit your rough drafts to show where you made a mistake in your writing.

Proofreading marks are a shortcut way of writing. They will save you time when you are editing and proofreading your work. Here are some proofreading marks to use.

¶	Indent the paragraph.
≡	Make a capital letter.
/	Make a lowercase letter.
"sp"	Check spelling.
^	Add something.
℅	Take out something.
⊙	Add a period.
˄	Add a comma.

Frankie is editing his story about someone from a different planet. Here is what he has done so far.

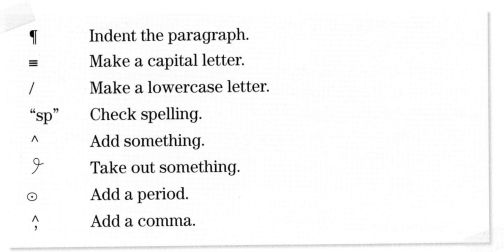

> sp
> Glimo did not walk. He (roled).
>
> that sent out sparks
> Where our toes would be, he had blue wheels.
>
> sp
> It was (wunderfull) to /see him move.
>
> great
> He looked like a ~~big~~ blue streak.

Evaluating and Revising

Do you like to read reports that are not organized? No one does. Yet it takes time and thinking to organize a piece of writing. It also takes practice to see ways to improve your writing.

After writing your first draft, you can often find ways to improve it. Maybe you will change the order of two paragraphs. Maybe you will break a long sentence into two shorter, clearer ones. Maybe you will combine two short, choppy sentences.

Sometimes it is hard to know when your writing is the best it can be. When can you stop making revisions?

SECTION 3

Writing Strategies

The list of questions on the next page can help. They are grouped by topic, just as facts should be grouped by topic in your reports. After you write your first draft, ask yourself each question. Then carefully check your writing before you answer it. When you can answer "yes" to every question, your writing is ready for readers.

It helps to put a project away overnight or at least for a few hours. When you read it again, your brain will be fresh. You will be more likely to see ways to improve your writing. If possible, trade drafts with a partner. You can help each other spot problems and find ways to fix them.

Organization

▶ Does my writing have a beginning, a middle, and an end?

▶ Does my introduction (beginning) tell my topic? Does it make people want to keep reading?

▶ Are the ideas in the middle in logical order? It might be:

  ▶ cause and effect, telling what caused what
  ▶ compare and contrast, telling how two things are the same and different
  ▶ time order, telling events in the order they happened
  ▶ main idea and details, dividing the main topic into smaller topics

▶ Does my ending restate my main points?

▶ Does each paragraph have a topic sentence?

▶ Do transition words help show the order of events?

SECTION

3

Writing
Strategies

Ideas

▶ Do I stay on the topic?

▶ Are my ideas clear?

▶ Do my descriptions paint pictures in the reader's mind?

Vocabulary

▶ Did I choose my words carefully?

▶ Do I use some pronouns and synonyms instead of repeating words?

▶ Do I use action words and concrete adjectives?

Sentence Fluency

▶ Does each sentence lead smoothly to the next one?

▶ Are my sentences all complete?

▶ Do my sentences start in different ways?

▶ Are my sentences different lengths?

Voice

▶ Can readers tell that I am interested in this topic?

Presentation

Presentation is the last big step in the writing process. You have worked very hard to make your writing sound good, to have good sentences, to make sense, and to be correct with facts and information. Now it is time to make it *look* good! Make sure your final draft is neatly written or typed. Add pictures or other illustrations. Think about publishing your writing in the school paper. When you present your writing in a pleasing way, people will want to read it.

SECTION

3

Writing
Strategies

In addition to neatly writing or typing your work, you should add graphics to help illustrate and clarify the text. Use some of the following sources to illustrate your writing.

- Drawings
- Photographs
- Diagrams
- Maps
- Charts
- Tables

Try It!

Which type of media would be helpful to illustrate ideas for each topic? Continue reading this section of the Handbook to find out more information about presenting your writing.

- An informative report on snakes
- Directions to the library
- A list of favorite colors
- A play about a wicked queen
- A newspaper article about school lunches

SECTION

3

Writing
Strategies

Illustration

Illustration

Illustrating your writing can make your writing more clear. Illustrations also make your work look interesting. There are many types of illustrations. There are:

drawings	photographs	diagrams
graphs	charts	tables

The kind of illustration you choose will depend on what you are writing. No matter what kind you choose, remember to write a caption to go with it. A caption tells readers what you want them to know about the illustration.

SECTION

3

Writing
Strategies

Drawings and Photographs

Drawings and photographs show pictures of someone or something. They usually do not have words. Suppose you are writing a biography of your favorite author. Your biography will be more interesting if you include a photograph of him or her. If you are writing a trickster tale, you could draw a picture to illustrate your tale. Don't forget to add a caption.

Diagrams and Maps

Diagrams and maps usually have words and pictures. *Diagrams* often show the parts of something. For example, you could make a diagram to show the parts of a tree. A *map* shows places. There are many kinds of maps. You can find maps of cities, countries, and even of the sky.

Charts and Tables

Charts and tables usually just have words. They are helpful to use when you are comparing or listing information. Suppose you are writing about whales and dolphins. You might make a chart that shows how long the animals are and how much they weigh, or how they are alike and how they are different.

Where to Find Illustrations

Look in books, magazines, newspapers, and old calendars. The Internet is also a good place to look. Your teacher or a librarian can help you find Web sites with illustrations that are just right for students. You can also take your own photographs or make your own drawings to illustrate your writing.

SECTION

3

Writing
Strategies

Presentation and Publication

Presentation

Presenting your writing is an exciting part of the writing process. There are many ways to present your writing.

For an informative report

▷ find photographs to help illustrate your main idea
▷ use a chart or a graph that shows factual details
▷ give a presentation in class, showing your graph or chart

For a book review

▷ create a cover drawing that illustrates your favorite scene from the book
▷ add other drawings inside that show different parts of the book you reviewed

For a poem or short story

▷ find or create a drawing to go with your writing
▷ practice reading your writing aloud; then read it to your class
▷ create a book of poems or short stories
▷ send your stories and poems to a magazine to be published
▷ record your writing; that way your audience can read *and* hear your writing at the same time

SECTION

3

Writing
Strategies

Publication

There are plenty of places to publish your writing. Many schools have a school newspaper, a student bulletin board, or a school newsletter where they publish student writing and art. If your school doesn't have a newspaper you might make your own book, start a student magazine, or a student newspaper. If you wrote a letter, be sure to send it. You could also make a slide show or a video to show to your class or your family.

EXAMPLE Lucy wrote a poem about fall leaves. What could Lucy add to her poem in order to enhance the presentation of her poem?

Fall Leaves
By Lucy Levin

The leaves start to fall
    when it gets cold.
Some are scarlet,
    and some are gold.
They fall to the ground,
    and they sail in the air.
They skitter and scatter
    everywhere.

Does your school have its own Web site? You could publish your writing there. If you publish your writing on a Web site, you could add fun details to your Web presentation, such as:

a slide show	a video
sounds	music
pictures	Web links

EXAMPLE Tonio wrote a report on whales. He is publishing his report on the school Web site.

Humpback Whales

By Tonio Thomas

Humpback whales are very large. They are about 48 feet long. That is about as long as five cars put together. Humpbacks weigh between 25 and 40 tons.

Humpbacks live in every ocean in the world, but they act the same wherever they live. They can jump in the air and then dive back in the water. This is called breaching. They also sing songs to each other. It is their way of talking.

Someday I hope I get to see a humpback.

Publish with Others

Sometimes you can work with other students to publish your work. You could make a class book. Each one of you can add a story. You can decide together what the covers should look like.

If you have written a play, other students could help you perform it. They could be actors, or they could help make the scenery. You could videotape your play and make it look like a television show. You could even make it a puppet show.

Newspapers and magazines are also fun to work on with other students. Decide together how you can make your newspaper or magazine look real. You will probably need to do research at the library to find out more about successful magazines and newspapers.

Try It!

Study the way a magazine or newspaper looks. Find two things you could do to make your own magazine or newspaper look real.

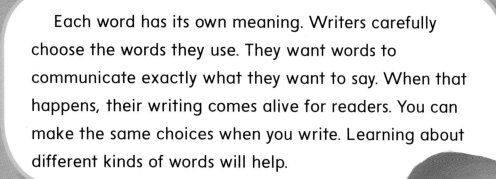

Each word has its own meaning. Writers carefully choose the words they use. They want words to communicate exactly what they want to say. When that happens, their writing comes alive for readers. You can make the same choices when you write. Learning about different kinds of words will help.

Temporal Words

Time Words

Time words tell when things happen. *Last night, this morning, yesterday, tomorrow, next Saturday,* and *today* are time words.

Order Words

Order words tell in what order things happen. *First, then, next, after, later,* and *finally* are order words.

Time and order words help you organize your writing and make your writing easier to follow and understand.

SECTION

4

Vocabulary

EXAMPLE Amy wrote in her journal about her trip to her grandparents' farm. She used time and order words to help organize her story.

> Last month my family took a trip to my grandparents' farm. We left early in the morning so we could get there by dinnertime. Dad had to drive all day Friday. Then he slept all day Saturday! We had planned to stay until the next weekend, and we almost did.
>
> Mom's hay fever started right away, though. Then, my little brother broke his arm on Monday. Every morning at 5:00 a.m., the roosters woke us up. Dad said we had to go home before anything else happened!

EXAMPLE Jeremy wrote about a science project in his class. Here is part of his report. He used order words to help organize his explanation.

First we got a tall jar and made a papier-mâché mountain around it. After the mountain was dry, we painted it. Then we glued twigs on it to look like trees. Finally, we were ready to explode the volcano.

Try It!

There are time and order words in the sentences below. See if you can find them all.

Last year I was in the second grade, and I was the shortest kid in my class. This week, we finally got a new kid who is shorter than I am!

Reading Your Writing

Knowing words that show time and order will help you keep track of the order of events as you write. Using these signal words will also help make your writing easier to follow and understand.

SECTION

4

Vocabulary

Place and Location Words

Place and **location** words show where people or things are. These words can also show where the action is happening. *Above, across, at, behind, below, beside, between, by, down, in, next to, on, over, through, up,* and *under* are place and location words.

> *We took the long way home today.*
>
> *We took the long way, down the road beside the river and through the woods, to get home today.*

The first sentence tells just a fact. The second sentence uses place and location words to give a clear picture of *the long way home.*

EXAMPLE Tara wrote a newspaper article about helping pack the car for a family camping trip. She used place and location words to tell where everything was.

Pack It Up!

Here's how to pack a car for a camping trip. First we pack the backpacks in the back. Sleeping bags go on top of the backpacks. We put the tent over the sleeping bags. Games and books are packed under the seats.

Try It!

What place and location words and phrases can you add to the two sentences below to make them clearer?

under the table	*across the street*
behind the sofa	*up in the tree*
on the shelf	*in a box*

I looked for my kitten.

I finally found her.

Using place and location words helps you communicate with your readers in two ways.

Ideas: Place and location words help give readers a clear picture of where people, things, and actions are.

Word Choice: Choosing the right place and location words helps readers understand your writing.

Writing Connection

You can use words that show place and location as you write to show where people or things are or where something is happening. This will help your readers understand your writing.

SECTION

4

Vocabulary

Compound Words

A **compound word** is made by putting two words together to form one word. Sometimes you can figure out the meaning of a compound word by looking at the two words that form it.

every + one = everyone

A compound word doesn't always take its meaning from the words that form it.

under + stand = understand

high + way = highway

Try It!

Name a compound word that could replace each of the following phrases.

▶ house for a dog
▶ coat you wear in the rain
▶ knob on a door
▶ corn made for popping

Writing Connection

A compound word is made by joining two smaller words. Look in a dictionary to make sure the compound word you are using is spelled correctly.

Antonyms

An **antonym** is a word that means the opposite or nearly the opposite of another word. Words such as *hot* and *cold* are antonyms.

You can use antonyms in your writing to show a difference between two things.

Here are some antonyms you might use in your writing.

right—left	*early—late*	*before—after*
wild—tame	*close—open*	*wet—dry*
lost—found	*rough—smooth*	*short—long*

Try It!

Think of an antonym for each word below.

full   day   push

Writing Connection

Antonyms are words with opposite meanings. Use antonyms to point out differences.

SECTION

4

Vocabulary

Synonyms

A **synonym** is a word that has the same or almost the same meaning as another word. The words *sad, unhappy,* and *gloomy* are synonyms.

When you use the same words again and again, your readers can become bored. Using different words to say the same thing or to make your message clearer helps keep your reader interested. Here is an example.

Instead of saying: *Jasmine saw a big spider.*

You might say: *Jasmine saw an enormous spider.*

Here are some other synonyms you could use in your writing.

hard—difficult	*task—chore*	*yell—shout*
seem—appear	*story—tale*	*right—correct*
sick—ill	*mistake—error*	*cry—weep*

Try It!

Think of a synonym for each of these words.

happy   angry   tired

Writing Connection

Synonyms are words with similar meanings. Using synonyms helps make your writing more interesting.

Adjectives

An **adjective** is a word that adds information to a noun or a pronoun. Adjectives tell how something looks, feels, smells, sounds, or tastes. They also tell how many or how much. Using adjectives helps your reader imagine what you are describing.

Good: *I have a pencil.*

Better: *I have a **shiny blue** pencil with a **sharp** point.*

Here are some other adjectives you might use in your writing.

Looks	Smells	Tastes	Sounds	Feels
small	sweet	sour	squeaky	wet
green	stinky	spicy	quiet	slimy
round	clean	bitter	clanging	smooth
bright	musty	sweet	noisy	fuzzy

SECTION

4

Vocabulary

Try It!

Think of adjectives to describe a dog.

Writing Connection

An adjective adds information to a noun or pronoun. Adjectives can help your reader picture or sense the things you describe.

Homophones

Homophones are words that sound the same but have different spellings and meanings. Words such as *ate* and *eight* are homophones. *Ate* is the past tense of *eat*. *Eight* is a number that is one more than seven.

Knowing the meanings of homophones will help you choose the correct words when you are writing.

If you are not sure which spelling is the right one, look up the words in a dictionary and read their meanings.

Here is a list of homophones and their meanings. Notice how each one is used in a sentence.

by—near *buy*—to pay for something	*The room is* by *the library.* *I will* buy *my lunch today.*
hear—to listen *here*—at or in this place	*I* hear *someone singing.* *Will you be* here *tomorrow?*
hole—an opening *whole*—entire	*I have a* hole *in my shoe.* *I ate the* whole *sandwich.*
right—correct; right direction *write*—make marks on paper	*The car turned* right. *I will* write *a story.*
their—possessive pronoun *there*—at another place *they're*—they are	*What is* their *last name?* *Put the box over* there. They're *leaving now.*
to—in the direction of *too*—also; very *two*—number	*Throw* to *first base.* *I want to go* too. *I am* too *hot.* *I have* two *books.*
your—possessive pronoun *you're*—you are	*Are these* your *pencils?* You're *my best friend.*
its—possessive pronoun *it's*—it is	*The bird is in* its *cage.* It's *singing sweetly.*

Try It!

Think of sentences using the homophones *pear* and *pair*.

Writing Connection

Homophones sound the same but have different meanings and spellings. Look up a homophone in the dictionary to make sure you use the correct word. Choosing the wrong homophone could confuse your readers.

Homographs

Many words are spelled the same but have more than one meaning. For example, a *bat* can be a flying animal or it may be a stick used to hit a baseball. Here are some more words that are spelled and sound the same but have different meanings.

batter—one who hits a ball	*batter*—liquid baking mixture
fly—an insect	*fly*—go through the air
bill—money owed	*bill*—bird's beak
gum—sticky stuff from trees	*gum*—body tissue around teeth
ear—body part used for hearing	*ear*—part of a corn plant
story—something you read or tell	*story*—a level of a building
fan—machine for moving air	*fan*—a supporter of a sports team

When you are writing, be sure to give your readers enough information to know which word you are using. For example, if you write *I saw a fan*, it is not clear which fan you mean. If you give your reader more information by writing *I saw a fan yelling during the game*, then your reader knows you mean someone who supports a team.

More Words with More Than One Meaning

Some words that are spelled the same are both pronounced differently and mean different things. For example, *bow* can be pronounced with a long *o* sound and mean "a ribbon on a package." It can rhyme with *cow* and mean "to bend from the waist."

Here are some words you might use in your writing.

live (long *i*)—having life *live* (short *i*)—to exist	That is a *live* frog. Do you *live* here?
wind (long *i*)—to turn *wind* (short *i*)—moving air	*Wind* the clock. The *wind* blew.

Try It!

Make up sentences using some of the words on page 326 to show their meaning.

Writing Connection

Be aware of words that are spelled the same but have different meanings. They may be pronounced the same way or differently. When you use them in your writing, it is important to give your reader enough information to know which word you are using.

Prefixes

A **prefix** is a word part added to the beginning of a word, changing the meaning. The prefix *re-* means "again." Adding *re-* to the base word *write* makes the word *rewrite,* which means "to write again."

Some prefixes have more than one meaning. Here are some common prefixes and their meanings.

Prefix	Meaning	Example
re-	again	repaint
un-	not, opposite, reverse action	unhappy, unable, unlock
dis-	not, opposite	disagree
mis-	bad or wrong	misspell
over-	too much	overcooked
bi-	two	bicycle
tri-	three	triangle
pre-	before	preschool

Try It!

What prefix would you add to *appear* to make a word that means "to appear again"?

Writing Connection

A prefix is added to the beginning of a word and changes its meaning. Learning and using prefixes will help you add to your vocabulary.

Suffixes

A **suffix** is a word part that is added to the end of a word and changes its meaning. For example, the suffix *-ful* means "full of." Adding *-ful* to the base word *fear* makes the word *fearful,* which means "full of fear."

Use suffixes to make words that tell the reader exactly what you want to say. Here are some suffixes and their meanings.

Suffix	Meaning	Example
-ful	full of	joyful
-less	without	careless
-er, -or	one who does	teacher, actor
-ness	state or quality of	darkness
-y	being or having	dirty
-ly	like	fatherly

Try It!

Combine each base word and suffix. What is the meaning of the new word?

　　hope + *ful*　　　honest + *ly*　　　work + *er*

Writing Connection

A suffix is added to the end of a word and changes its meaning. If you aren't sure what a suffix means, look it up in the dictionary.

SECTION

4

Vocabulary

Context Clues

How do you figure out the meaning of a new word that you find when you are reading? One way is to use **context clues.** Context clues are found in the words and sentences near the unfamiliar word. Pictures can also give context clues that help you figure out a word's meaning.

Look at this example from "Storm Chasers" by Alanna Parker.

A tornado that occurs over water is called a waterspout. In the United States, they are most frequently found off the coast of Florida, but can also be seen regularly on the Great Lakes. Waterspouts are a serious hazard, and just like with tornados over land, people need to take precautions to avoid them.

You may not know what the word *hazard* means, but there are clues in the paragraph if you don't. The paragraph says that people need to take precautions to avoid the hazard. This tells me that hazards must be some type of danger or threat.

Sometimes context clues come right after the word. Here is an example sentence with the definition right next to the difficult word.

Tara looked <u>agitated,</u> **or nervous,** when she gave her speech to the committee.

SECTION

4

Vocabulary

Try It!

Use context clues to figure out the meaning of the underlined word in each sentence below.

An adjective <u>modifies,</u> or describes, a noun or pronoun.

There was an <u>error,</u> or mistake, on my paper.

The cloth was <u>moist,</u> not dry, when he touched it.

Tips for Understanding New Words

▶ Keep reading. Look for clues in the words and sentences near the new word.

▶ Look for context clues in pictures.

Writing Connection

Context clues help a reader figure out the meaning of a new word. Include context clues in your writing if you use words that readers might not know.

Apposition

Apposition is a shortcut that writers use to make their writing sound smoother. Good writers use apposition when they put words that tell more about a subject next to the subject in the same sentence.

Here is an example. Suppose you were talking about your dog. You could say

> My dog likes to play. He is the one with the red collar.

However, this is a better way to say it.

> My dog, the one with the red collar, likes to play.

The words *the one with the red collar* are in apposition to the words *my dog*. Notice the words that were cut out of the second sentence. Also notice the commas that were added. Often, you use commas around the words that are in apposition.

Try It!

Darla wrote the sentences below.
   Dandelions are the yellow flowers growing in the grass.
   They make me sneeze.
How might you change them by using apposition?

Word Analysis

Looking at the structure of a word is what good readers and writers do to figure out the different parts that make up a word. **Word analysis** is how a word is put together and what the different parts of a word mean.

Here are some examples of different word structures.

Greek Roots

dec means "ten" **decade**

grat means "thankful" **grateful**

scope means "to see" **microscope**

Latin Roots

loc means "place" **location**

ped means "foot" **pedal**

scrib means "to write" **scribble**

Base Words and Affixes

base word *paint* + affix   **repaint   painted   painting   painter   unpainted**

Word Family

root word *act*   **action   react   active   acting   acted   actress   activity   inaction**

SECTION
4
Vocabulary

Try It!

Here are four words in a word family. What is the base word? Name two more words in the family.

movie   unmoved   movable   moved

Across-the-Curriculum Words

You will probably read many new words in books about math, science, social studies, and health. Learning these words will help you understand what you read. You can also use them in your writing.

Here is a list of words you might find in these subjects. A definition is given for each word.

Math

addition—combining numbers into one sum

decimal—relating to or based on the number *ten*

difference—the number that is left after subtracting one quantity from another

divide—to separate or arrange into groups

estimate—to make a rough judgment or calculation of

fraction—one or more of the equal parts of a whole

graph—a diagram showing the changes of and relationship between two or more elements

order—to arrange by size or amount

place value—the value given to a digit, based on the position it has in a number

sum—the answer obtained from adding numbers

Science

amphibian—cold-blooded vertebrates (including frogs, toads, and salamanders) usually living in or near water

cell—the basic unit of all living things

dissolve—to cause to pass into solution with a liquid

energy—the ability to do work

erosion—the gradual wearing or washing away of the soil and rock of the earth's surface by glaciers, waves, running water, or wind

friction—the force that resists motion between two surfaces that are touching

gravity—the force that the earth exerts on bodies at or near its surface

hypothesis—an unproved explanation based on known facts

recycle—to use again

SECTION

4

Vocabulary

Social Studies

artifact—something made and left behind by people
who lived long ago

barter—to trade (goods or services) without using money

Capitol—the building in Washington, D.C., where the U.S.
Congress meets

consumer—a person who buys goods and services

country—a nation or independent state

culture—the way of life of a group of people, including
their common language, social institutions,
customs, beliefs, and art

equator—an imaginary line around the center of the Earth
halfway between the North and South Poles

explorer—a person who travels to collect information
about geography or science

producer—a person or group that makes goods or provides
services

rural—relating to the country or country life

urban—relating to a city or city life

SECTION 4

Vocabulary

Health

bacteria—one-celled organisms that may help or hurt a host

digestion—the process by which food is broken down and used by the body

disease—illness

infection—an attack on part of the body by bacteria, viruses, or fungi whose growth causes disease

medicine—a drug or other substance used to treat disease or relieve pain

stress—mental or physical tension or pressure

Try It!

Use one word from each subject area in a sentence.

Writing Connection

Learning words that are used in different subjects can help you better understand what you read. You might also use these words when you write your own stories and reports.

SECTION
4

Vocabulary

SECTION 5

Grammar, Usage, and Mechanics

You know about rules. When you know and follow the rules of a game, you're better at the game. It's the same with writing. Knowing the rules and following them will make you a better writer.

Grammar

Grammar is about how language is organized. Parts of speech, such as nouns and verbs, are grammar. The names for different parts of a sentence are grammar. Knowing about grammar helps you understand how to build sentences that make sense to your readers.

The rules of grammar tell you about the following concepts:

- Nouns
- Pronouns
- Verbs
- Adjectives and Adverbs
- Prepositions and Prepositional Phrases
- Conjunctions
- Sentences
- Paragraphs

EXAMPLE

Fragment: Ran home.

Sentence: Allie ran home.

Fragment: My dog.

Sentence: My dog barks a lot.

Continue reading this section of the Handbook to see more examples and to find out additional information about the rules of grammar.

SECTION

5

Grammar,
Usage, and
Mechanics

Nouns

Nouns name everything. For example, **nouns** are words that name people, places, things, and ideas.

| boy | zoo | balloons | time |

Common nouns name any person, place, thing, or idea. Common nouns start with a lowercase letter. **Proper nouns** name specific people, places, things, or ideas. Proper nouns start with a capital letter.

Common nouns: girl, park, skyscraper, nationality

Proper nouns: Megan, Yellowstone Park, Willis Tower, Cuba

Singular and Plural Nouns

A **singular noun** names one person, place, or thing. A **plural noun** names more than one person, place, or thing.

▶ **Regular plural nouns** are formed by adding *-s*, *-es*, or *-ies* to singular nouns.

| dog **dogs** | box **boxes** | baby **babies** |

▶ **Irregular plural nouns** do not follow the rules for forming regular plural nouns. Rules for forming irregular plural nouns vary. Check the dictionary for the correct spelling of irregular plural nouns. Below are some examples.

| child | **children** | tooth | **teeth** |
| man | **men** | deer | **deer** |

Abstract Nouns

An **abstract noun** is something that you cannot experience with your five senses. Abstract nouns are feelings, concepts, and ideas.

kindness   honesty   childhood   knowledge   love

Possessive Nouns

Possessive nouns show who has or owns something.

Grandpa's blue eyes   the **raccoon's** tail
a **firefighter's** hat   the **room's** doors

Singular possessive nouns are formed by adding an apostrophe (') plus *s* to singular nouns. **Plural possessive nouns** can be formed in two ways. When a plural noun ends with *s*, an apostrophe is added to form the possessive plural noun. When a plural noun does not end with *s*, an apostrophe plus *s* is added to form the possessive plural noun.

Singular Possessive Nouns

robin + 's = robin's   the **robin's** nest

Plural Possessive Nouns

players + ' = players'   the **players'** baseball gloves
women + 's = women's   the **women's** offices

Pronouns

Pronouns are words that take the place of nouns. Personal pronouns refer to people or things.

Olivia loves to swim.	**She** loves to swim.
Yusef bought **the poster**.	Yusef bought **it**.
The Lions won the game.	**They** won the game.
Mustafa brought **Tracie and me** a pizza.	Mustafa brought **us** a pizza.

Pronouns can be singular or plural.

Singular	I, me, you, he, him, she, her, it
Plural	we, us, they, them, you

Tyler (singular noun) likes to ride *his bike* (singular noun).

He (singular pronoun) likes to ride *it* (singular pronoun).

My sisters (plural noun) like to play with *Sam* (singular noun).

They (plural pronoun) like to play with *him* (singular pronoun).

Try It!

Which of the five possessive nouns in the sentence below are singular? Which are plural?

Tyler's dad brought the students' sweaters from the teacher's van to the third graders' bench at the Children's Kite-Flying Contest.

Possessive Pronouns

A **possessive pronoun** shows who owns something. Possessive pronouns take the place of possessive nouns and can be singular or plural. Possessive pronouns do not have apostrophes. Some possessive pronouns are used before nouns. Others are used alone.

children's song	**Jane's** brother	**Min's** book
their song	**her** brother	**his** book
our cat	**my** bike	**their** car
the cat is **ours**	the bike is **mine**	the car is **theirs**

Here are all of the singular and plural possessive pronouns.

	Used Before Nouns	Used Alone
Singular	my your its her his	mine yours its hers his
Plural	our their your	ours theirs yours

Try It!

There are three possessive pronouns in the sentences below. Can you find them all?

My book is red, and her book is blue. Kevin thought the blue one was mine.

SECTION

5

Grammar,
Usage, and
Mechanics

Verbs

There are different types of verbs. An **action verb** tells about an action of something or someone in a sentence. Actions can be seen or unseen.

Seen action: The dog **ran** all the way home.

Unseen action: Alex **forgot** his library book.

A **state-of-being verb** does not tell about an action. It tells about a condition or a state of being.

Our friends **were** here for a visit.

When a state-of-being verb connects the subject of a sentence with a word in the predicate, the verb is a **linking verb**.

I **am** a student.   My aunt **is** a teacher.

You **are** a good cook.   Josh **was** helpful with the baby.

A **verb phrase** is one or more **helping verbs** followed by the **main verb**. Helping verbs help the main verb express an action or state of being.

She **has won** the race. (helping verb+main verb)

She **could have won** the race. (two helping verbs+main verb)

Forms of *Be* and *Have*

The verb **be** does not show the action of someone or something in a sentence. It is a state-of-being verb. It tells what someone or something is or is like. There are different forms of the verb *be*.

am	are	is	was	were	being	been

Forms of *be* can be used as linking verbs.

The team **is** unbeaten.
The dog **was** lost.
The Carson twins **were** my friends.

Forms of *be* can also be used as helping verbs and as main verbs.

I **am** walking. (helping verb)
They **were** writing. (helping verb)
She has **been** here. (main verb)

The verb **have** can be used as a main verb or as a helping verb.

have	has	had

She **has** a kitten. (main verb)
The kittens **have become** playful. (helping verb)
My mother **has decided** to keep them. (helping verb)

SECTION

5

Grammar, Usage, and Mechanics

Adjectives

Adjectives describe a noun or a pronoun. Adjectives tell what kind, how many, and which one.

What Kind	How Many	Which One
blue	three	this
long	many	that
furry	few	these
good	some	those

Proper adjectives are made from proper nouns. Like proper nouns, proper adjectives always start with a capital letter.

American flag   *Chinese* food   *Spanish* folksongs

Articles

Articles are a special group of adjectives. *A* and *an* are **indefinite articles**. They refer to a general group of people, places, things, or ideas.

A is used before words that begin with a consonant sound.

a dog   *a* house   *a* card

An is used before words that begin with a vowel sound.

an egg   *an* hour   *an* apple

The is a **definite article**. It identifies specific people, places, things, or ideas.

the book   *the* door   *the* cat

Adverbs

An **adverb** is a word that describes a verb, an adjective, or another adverb. An adverb tells how, when, where, or how much something happens.

How	When	Where	How Much
carefully	now	here	very
fast	again	outside	nearly
neatly	often	everywhere	greatly

An adverb can be placed in different parts of a sentence. It can come before the verb, after the verb, at the beginning of the sentence, or at the end of the sentence.

Before the Verb	We **often** play at the park.
After the Verb	We play **often** at the park.
At the Beginning of the Sentence	**Often**, we play at the park.
At the End of the Sentence	We play at the park **often**.

Try It!

Find five adverbs in the sentences below.

My baby sister is a sight at mealtime. She gets soggy crackers in her hair, mashed bananas here and there, and orange juice everywhere! She is happily learning to wear her food.

SECTION

5

Grammar, Usage, and Mechanics

Prepositions and Prepositional Phrases

A **preposition** is a word that tells about the position or direction of a noun or pronoun.

Common Prepositions

about	above	across	after	against
along	around	at	before	behind
below	beside	between	by	down
for	from	in	inside	into
like	near	of	off	on
out	outside	over	through	to
under	underneath	up	with	without

A preposition is needed to begin a group of words called a prepositional phrase. A **prepositional phrase** begins with a preposition and ends with a noun or pronoun. You will use prepositions in your writing to show where something is or where it is going.

The dog ran **down the road**.

Keisha is **across the street**.

Try It!

How many of the prepositions in the list above fit in the sentence below?

The rabbit jumped _____ the log.

Conjunctions

A **conjunction** is a joining or connecting word. **Coordinating conjunctions** connect words or phrases. The most common coordinating conjunctions are *and, or, but,* and *so.*

It's raining ***cats and dogs***.

Would you like ***soup or salad?***

Marc ***made and sold*** his own cards.

Do you like ***red or blue*** better?

I play ***soccer but not basketball***.

Subordinating conjunctions connect two clauses that are not equal. The clause that cannot stand alone contains the subordinating conjunction. Some common subordinating conjunctions are *although, until, because, unless, since, if,* and *while.*

Since you cleaned your room, you can watch a movie tonight.

Unless you finish your homework, you can't go outside to play.

Because it is raining, I will wear my raincoat.

If my mom agrees, I will come to your party.

SECTION

5

Grammar, Usage, and Mechanics

Sentences

A **sentence** has two parts, a **subject** and a **predicate**. The subject names the person or thing the sentence is about. The predicate tells what the subject is or does. The predicate may be a verb only or a verb plus other words. A sentence always begins with a capital letter and ends with a punctuation mark.

EXAMPLE

Jenny played a game.

The subject is *Jenny*. It tells what the sentence is about. The predicate is *played a game*. It tells what Jenny did.

Elijah is happy.

This sentence is about Elijah. The subject is *Elijah*. The predicate is *is happy*. It tells what Elijah is.

Try It!

Find the subject and predicate in this sentence:
    My friends play games.

SECTION

5

Grammar, Usage, and Mechanics

Subjects and Predicates

Every sentence has a subject and a predicate. The **complete subject** is all the words that tell whom or what a sentence is about. The **simple subject** is the noun that tells who or what does the action or is something in the sentence.

The brown dog lives in the city. (complete subject)

The brown **dog** lives in the city. (simple subject)

A **compound subject** is two or more simple subjects connected by a conjunction.

Mary and **Jack** live in the city.

My **mother** and **father** are doctors.

The **trees** and **buildings** are tall.

The **complete predicate** is all the words that tell what the subject is or does. The **simple predicate** is the verb that tells what the subject is or does.

They **live in the city**. (complete predicate)

They **live** in the city. (simple predicate)

A **compound predicate** is two or more predicates connected by a conjunction. A compound predicate tells two or more things about the subject.

They **live** and **work** in the city.

My parents **treat** and **cure** patients.

Direct Objects and Object Pronouns

A **direct object** in a sentence tells *what* or *who* received the action of the subject.

> Jamal bought pencils.

The subject is *Jamal*. The simple predicate is *bought*. The action (bought) has a receiver. *What* did Jamal buy? Jamal bought **pencils**. The word *pencils* is a direct object in the sentence because it tells *what* received the action of the subject.

An **object pronoun** is a pronoun acting as a direct object. Common object pronouns are *me, you, him, her, it, us, you,* and *them*.

> Jamal bought pencils.
> Jamal bought it.

In the second sentence the noun *pencils* has been replaced with the object pronoun *it*.

Try It!

Ask yourself the questions *what* or *whom* received the action of the subject in each sentence to identify the direct objects.

The dog fetches sticks.

A bee stung Sam.

My mom hugged me.

Kinds of Sentences

The four kinds of sentences are **declarative**, **interrogative**, **imperative**, and **exclamatory**. Sentences that tell something are statements, or declarative sentences. They end with a period. Sentences that ask something are questions, or interrogative sentences. They end in a question mark. Sentences that tell someone to do something are commands, or imperative sentences. They end with a period. Sentences that show strong feeling are exclamations, or exclamatory sentences. They end with an exclamation point.

EXAMPLE

Declarative: Jennifer likes to draw pictures.

Interrogative: What does Jennifer like to draw?

Imperative: Look at this picture.

Exclamatory: I love to draw!

Try It!

Change this interrogative sentence so that it is an imperative sentence.

Will you sit in this chair?

Reading Your Writing

Different kinds of sentences can be used to express your thoughts. Make sure you use the correct punctuation at the end of your sentences so you don't confuse your reader.

SECTION

5

Grammar, Usage, and Mechanics

Writing Sentences

Good sentences can be short or long, but you shouldn't use too many short sentences together. When writers use a lot of short sentences, they usually repeat words. Combining sentences and taking out the extra words will make your writing easier to read.

EXAMPLE

Leo likes fish.
He likes broccoli.
He likes milk.

The sentences are short and many words are repeated. You can get rid of the extra words by combining the sentences like this:

Leo likes fish, broccoli, and milk.

The longer sentence has the same meaning as the three short sentences but reads more smoothly.

Other parts of a sentence can be combined also.

Sam looks for crickets every day. Sam feeds his frog crickets every day.
Better: *Sam looks for crickets to feed his frog every day.*

Simple Sentences

Sentences can be formed in different ways. A **simple sentence** has one subject and one predicate. The subject of a simple sentence can be simple or compound. So can the predicate.

Simple Subject Earth	**Simple Predicate** **is** the third planet from the sun.
Compound Subject Neptune and Uranus	**Simple Predicate** **are** the farthest planets from the sun.
Simple Subject The sun	**Compound Predicate** **shines** light and **sends** heat to Earth.
Compound Subject Venus and Mars	**Compound Predicate** have been **photographed** and **mapped** by scientists.

Compound and Complex Sentences

Compound Sentences

A **compound sentence** is two or more simple sentences joined by a conjunction. A comma is placed before the conjunction in a compound sentence.

Use *and* to join two sentences that contain similar ideas.

Use *but* to join sentences that are on the same topic but contain different ideas.

Use *or* to join sentences that are related but show a choice between two ideas.

Tia wrote the story, **and** Peter drew the illustrations.

The story is sad, **but** the pictures are beautiful.

Are Tia and Peter finished, **or** are they going to add a cover?

Complex Sentences

A **complex sentence** is made of an independent clause and one or more dependent clauses. An independent clause can stand alone as a sentence, but a dependent clause cannot. To rewrite two sentences as a complex sentence, make the idea from one of the sentences a dependent clause. A dependent clause begins with a subordinating conjunction such as *although, until, because, unless, since, if,* and *while.* Other words, such as *which* and *who,* are also used to introduce the dependent clause in a complex sentence.

Tia has high hopes. She worked so hard on her story.

Tia has high hopes because she worked so hard on her story.

Sentence Problems

1. **Fragment:** A group of words that is missing a subject, a predicate, or both.
2. **Run-on:** Two or more sentences that are put together without a conjunction, such as *and* or *but*.
3. **Rambling:** A sentence that has a lot of conjunctions. The conjunctions join sentences that should be written separately.

EXAMPLE

Fragment: *Ran fast.*
Sentence: *Marcus ran fast.*

Run-on: *My sister's name is Ramona she's a pest.*
Better: *My sister's name is Ramona, and she's a pest.*

Rambling: *My brothers and I went camping and hiked in the woods and swam in the lake and slept in a tent.*
Better: *My brothers and I went camping. We hiked in the woods and swam in the lake. Later, we slept in a tent.*

Try It!

How could you fix this run-on sentence?
I like the weekend my favorite day is Saturday.

Paragraphs

A **paragraph** is one or more sentences that tell about the same thing. All of the sentences go together to tell about one main idea.

Many paragraphs have a topic sentence, supporting sentences, and a closing sentence. A **topic sentence** tells the main idea. Often, the topic sentence is the first sentence in the paragraph. **Supporting sentences** tell more about the idea in the topic sentence. A closing sentence can be a summary, or it can provide a closing thought. With each new idea, a writer should begin a new paragraph. The first line of each paragraph is indented. This tells the reader where paragraphs begin and end.

> **EXAMPLE** Read this paragraph. The topic sentence is underlined. Notice how all of the sentences tell more about what makes Mona a good writer.
>
> Mona is a very good writer. She uses a graphic organizer to plan her writing. Then she uses it to write a draft. After thinking about the draft for a day or two, Mona revises and edits it. Mona puts a lot of work into her writing.

Staying on the Topic

All of the sentences in a paragraph should be about the same idea. If you include a sentence that doesn't belong in the paragraph, readers might get confused.

EXAMPLE This paragraph doesn't stay on topic. The sentence that doesn't belong is crossed out. Read the paragraph with the sentence, then read it without.

Autumn is a beautiful time of year. ~~Spring is my favorite season~~. On the first day of autumn, day is the same length as night. Later, leaves fall to the ground, and animals prepare for winter.

Try It!

Which sentence in this paragraph doesn't belong?

The first day of summer is June 20 or 21. It has more hours of daylight than any other day of the year. My birthday is in June. There are about 15 1/2 hours of daylight on the first day of summer.

SECTION

5

Grammar, Usage, and Mechanics

Writing Paragraphs

You can write different kinds of paragraphs depending on your reason for writing. You might want to tell a story, describe something, explain something, or persuade someone.

Narrative

A **narrative** paragraph tells a story. The story can be real or make-believe. The purpose of a narrative paragraph is to entertain the reader.

EXAMPLE Andrew wrote this narrative paragraph to put on the writer's bulletin board in his classroom.

Topic ▶ Sentence	I thought today was going to be the worst day of my life. I woke up late and
Tell More ▶ About Topic Sentence	couldn't find my shoes. When I went to eat breakfast, there was no milk. I had to put water on my cereal. Then I couldn't find my backpack, so I missed the bus. Luckily, I had on my flying cape, and I made
Closing ▶ Sentence	it to school before the bell rang. It turned out to be a pretty good day after all.

Descriptive

A **descriptive** paragraph describes something in a way that forms a picture in the reader's mind. Using words that tell how something looks, smells, feels, sounds, or tastes helps create the picture.

EXAMPLE Here is Ethan's description of his dog.

Oliver is a great friend to me. He's a white, tan, and black beagle. He likes to sleep under my bed. Every morning Oliver wakes me up by flapping his ears and jingling the tags on his collar. He also licks my face with his rough, wet tongue. Oliver's bad breath wakes me up in a hurry! Thanks to Oliver I'm never lonely at night or late for school in the morning.

◀ Topic Sentence

◀ Details: How Oliver Looks, Sounds, Feels, Smells

◀ Closing Sentence

Try It!

Think of your trip to school this morning. What did you see, smell, hear, feel, or taste along the way?

SECTION

5

Grammar, Usage, and Mechanics

Informative

The purpose of an **informative** paragraph is to give information. It explains something that is real, not make-believe. Give examples or specific facts to make your ideas clear to your reader.

EXAMPLE Read this paragraph that Gina wrote. Notice how she gives examples to support her topic sentence.

Topic ▶ Sentence	Many different birds come to eat at our backyard birdfeeders. Yesterday I saw a
Examples ▶	cardinal, a blue jay, some sparrows, and a cowbird at our feeders. When the weather
Closing ▶ Sentence	gets colder, even more kinds of birds will come.

Now read this paragraph that Shandra wrote about sharks. In this paragraph, she gives facts about sharks that tell more about her topic sentence.

Topic ▶ Sentence	Sharks are very fast. Most of them swim 20 to 30 miles per hour. The mako
Facts ▶	shark can swim as fast as 60 miles per hour. Even the slowest shark can swim
Closing ▶ Sentence	faster than a person can.

Persuasive

A **persuasive** paragraph gives the writer's view on a topic and reasons or examples to support it. The writer's purpose is to persuade the reader to agree with him or her.

EXAMPLE Hanan wrote a persuasive paragraph for the school newspaper. She started with a question to interest her readers. Then, she answered the question in the rest of the paragraph.

> Why should we stop using foam food trays in the cafeteria? Every day about 400 kids eat a cafeteria lunch at our school. That means every day 400 foam trays are thrown away. They will be taken to a landfill. Foam trays never break down, so they will keep taking up more and more space. Trays that can be recycled or that will break down would be better choices.

◀ Question

◀ Support

◀ Closing Sentence

SECTION

5

Grammar, Usage, and Mechanics

Usage

Usage is about how we use language when we speak and write. For example, the rules of usage tell you when to use *is* and when to use *are*. They tell you when to use *taller* and when to use *tallest*. Learning the rules of usage will help people better understand what you say and what you write.

• •

SECTION

5

Grammar,
Usage, and
Mechanics

The rules of usage tell you about the following concepts:

▶ Verb Tenses
▶ Subject/Verb Agreement
▶ Forms of Adjectives and Adverbs
▶ Contractions

Verb Tenses

Present, Past, and Future Tenses

The **tense** of a verb tells when an action happens. Verbs in the **present tense** tell what is happening now or what happens all the time.

> She **walks** to school.
>
> Josh **is** hungry.

Verbs in the **past tense** tell what has already happened. The past tense of an action verb is often formed by adding *-ed* to the base form of the verb.

> She **walked** to school.
>
> Josh **was** hungry.

Verbs in the **future tense** tell what will happen later. The future tense is often formed with the helping verb *will*.

> We **will go** to the library on Thursday.

Regular and Irregular Verbs

Verbs can be regular or irregular. A **regular verb** is one whose past tense is formed by adding *-ed* to the base verb. When a regular verb ends with *e*, the *e* is dropped before adding *-ed*.

Present Tense	talk	jump	smile	bake
Past Tense	talked	jumped	smiled	baked

An **irregular verb** is one whose past tense is not formed by following the rule for adding *-ed* to the base verb. The spelling of an irregular verb changes to form the past tense. Some irregular verbs are spelled differently when they are used with the helping verbs *has*, *have*, and *had*.

Common Irregular Verbs					
Present Tense	am	are	is	begin	come
	do	draw	eat	fall	give
	go	has	have	make	run
	say	see	seek	take	write
Past Tense	was	were	began	came	did
	drew	ate	fell	gave	went
	had	made	ran	said	saw
	sought	took	wrote		
Past Tense with *has*, *have*, or *had*	been	begun	come	done	drawn
	eaten	fallen	given	gone	had
	made	run	said	seen	sought
	taken	written			

SECTION

5

Grammar, Usage, and Mechanics

Subject-Verb Agreement

The subject of a sentence must agree with its verb. They both must be either singular or plural.

When the subject is singular, or is a singular pronoun (*he, she,* or *it*), *-s* or *-es* is usually added to the base verb to form the present tense.

learn + s = learns	Anna **learns** quickly.
	She **learns** quickly.

When a verb ends with *ch, sh, s, x,* or *z*, *-es* is added to form the present tense.

wish + es = wishes	Bill **wishes** he could visit Alaska.

When a verb ends with a consonant and *y*, change the *y* to *i* and add *-es* to form the present tense.

study + es = studies	Kim **studies** every night.

When the subject is plural, or is a plural pronoun (*you, we,* or *they*), do not add *-s* or *-es* to the verb.

work	The students **work** well together.
	They **work** well together.

Irregular Verbs

Most past, present, and future tense **irregular verbs** are used with both singular and plural subjects. The **irregular verbs** *be* and *have* change forms to make the present tense. They must always agree with their subjects.

Verb	Tense	Singular Subject	Plural Subject
be	present past	James **is** here. James **was** here.	The kids **are** here. The kids **were** here.
have	present past	Christina **has** lunch. Christina **had** lunch.	The girls **have** lunch. The girls **had** lunch.

Subject-Verb Agreement with Compound Subjects

Compound subjects must agree with their verbs. A compound subject has two or more simple subjects that have the same verb. The rules for subject-verb agreement are different for different conjunctions.

When *and* is the conjunction, *-s* is not added to the verb.

The girls **and** boys **play** soccer together.
Alex **and** Julie **play** on the same team.

When *or* is the conjunction, look at both subjects. If they are singular, *-s* is added to the verb. If the subjects are plural, *-s* is not added to the verb.

Cats **or** dogs **make** good pets. (plural subjects)
A cat **or** a dog **makes** a good pet. (singular subjects)

SECTION

5

Grammar, Usage, and Mechanics

Forms of Adjectives and Adverbs

Some **adjectives** compare people, places, or things. A comparative adjective compares two people, places, or things.

Adjectives can compare one person, place, or thing with another. Add -*er* to most adjectives with one syllable. Use the word *more* before many adjectives with more than one syllable.

The lion is **faster** than the zebra.

Lions are **more graceful** than elephants.

Adjectives can compare three or more people, places, or things. Add -*est* to the end of most adjectives with one syllable. Use the word *most* before many adjectives with more than one syllable.

The cheetah is the **fastest** animal on land.

I think deer are the **most graceful** animals of all.

Some adjectives that compare have special forms.

Sue is a **better** singer than Rachel.

Grace is the **best** singer in the class.

Adverbs can compare actions. Add -*er* and -*est* to most short adverbs. Use *more* and *most* with adverbs ending in -*ly*.

Jan left **earlier** than Lee.

Kim left **earliest** of all.

Ben talked **more quietly** than Josh.

Ben talked **most quietly** of all.

Contractions

A **contraction** is a word made by joining two words and taking out one or more letters. An apostrophe shows where the letters are missing.

I am = I'm   they are = they're
you are = you're   I will = I'll
she is = she's   you will = you'll
it is = it's   he will = he'll
we are = we're   it will = it'll

Negative words are the word *no* and all words that mean *no*. Many contractions are negative words because they are made from the word *not*.

are not = aren't   had not = hadn't
will not = won't   cannot= can't
has not = hasn't   would not = wouldn't
is not = isn't   did not = didn't
do not = don't   should not = shouldn't
was not = wasn't   does not = doesn't

A **double negative** occurs when *two* negative words are used to express a single idea instead of *one* negative word. Many contractions use the negative word *not*. As a result, double negatives sometimes find their way into our speech and writing. Watch for the contraction trap, however, to avoid double negatives.

Incorrect: He does**n't** know **nothing** about karate.
  Correct: He doesn't know anything about karate.
  Correct: He knows nothing about karate.

Incorrect: We do**n't** have **no** lesson today.
  Correct: We don't have a lesson today.
  Correct: We have no lesson today.

SECTION

5

Grammar,
Usage, and
Mechanics

Mechanics

The rules of mechanics are very important in writing. How and when to use punctuation marks is part of mechanics. Knowing when to use capital letters is a part of mechanics. Writers who know and follow these rules make it much easier for readers to understand what they write.

The rules of mechanics tell you about the following concepts:

- End Marks
- Commas
- Quotation Marks
- Underlining
- Apostrophes
- Colons
- Hyphens
- Parentheses
- Capitalization

Try It!

Can you find the three mistakes in the sentences below?

- My family is going to the zoo on saturday.
- Do you have a dog!
- My mom bought lettuce carrots and apples at the store.

Continue reading this section of the Handbook to find out more information about the rules of mechanics.

SECTION

5

Grammar, Usage, and Mechanics

End Punctuation

Periods are used as end punctuation in sentences. Periods are also used in other ways.

▶ Periods end sentences that make statements.

February is the shortest month of the year.

▶ Periods end sentences that make demands or requests.

Please come to my party on Saturday.

▶ Periods are used after the initials in a person's name.

E. B. White wrote *Charlotte's Web* and *Stuart Little*.

▶ Periods are used after some abbreviations.

Jan. (January)   Mon. (Monday)

▶ Periods are used after abbreviations of people's titles.

Ms.   Mrs.   Mr.   Dr.   Jr.

▶ Periods are not used in some abbreviations where each letter stands for a word.

DVD (digital video disc)

Question marks are used to end sentences that ask questions.

Where is the library?
Do you have any brothers or sisters?

Exclamation points are used to end sentences that show strong feelings. Exclamation points are also used after interjections.

Wow! Please come back soon!

Commas

Commas are punctuation marks. They are used to separate words or set them off from the rest of the sentence.

▶ Commas are used between the name of a day and the year in a date.

Neil Armstrong walked on the moon on July 20, 1969.

▶ Commas are used between the names of a city and state or country.

Columbus, Ohio
Tokyo, Japan

▶ Commas are used after the greeting and the closing of a friendly letter.

Greetings: Dear Grandpa,   Dear Mary,
Closings: Your friend,   Truly,   With love,

▶ A comma is used between series of words or phrases.

We saw bison, moose, bears, and eagles in the park.

▶ A comma is used to set off the words of a speaker from other words in the sentence.

Dad said, "You earn money by raking the leaves."

▶ A comma is used after a person's name, after the words *yes* and *no*, and after a mild interjection at the beginning of a sentence.

Mom, can I have a pet snake?
Yes, when you have a house of your own.
Oh, that's a long time to wait.

▶ A comma is used before the conjunction in a compound sentence.

We sat on the porch swing, **and** we watched the sunset.

SECTION 5

Grammar, Usage, and Mechanics

Quotation Marks and Underlining

Quotation marks set off the exact words of a speaker or another writer. When you write, put quotation marks before and after the exact words of a speaker or writer. Use a comma to separate the exact words from the rest of the sentence. Place end punctuation for the exact words inside the quotation marks.

> Mom said patiently, "I'll wait right here for you."
> "Go, Zoe!" Dad yelled, "Score a goal!"

Quotation marks set off the titles of short stories, poems, songs, and the chapters of books.

> We always sing "Home on the Range" because our music teacher is from Kansas.
> I love the poems "Double-Tail Dog" and "Smart."

When you are writing, use **underlining** to set off the titles of books, magazines, newspapers, television shows, movies, and plays. Put these titles in italics if you are using a computer.

> Our teacher is reading *The Wind in the Willows* to our class.
> Mom bought the movie *Tarzan* because she liked it so much.
> The *International Trekkers* magazine for kids has great photos.

Apostrophes and Colons

An **apostrophe** is a punctuation mark used to make possessive nouns and contractions. Here are ways to use apostrophes to make possessive nouns.

▶ Add an apostrophe and -*s* to singular nouns.

Mom**'s** pancakes are the best.

▶ Add an apostrophe and -*s* to plural nouns that do not end in *s*.

We put our drawings in the Children's Art Show.

▶ Add only an apostrophe to plural nouns that end in *s*.

The students' gifts were collected.

▶ Add an apostrophe to show where letters have been left out in a contraction.

cannot = can't   I am = I'm   we will = we'll

A **colon** is a punctuation mark used to write hours and minutes. A colon is also used before a list in a sentence and after the greeting in a business letter.

▶ Use a colon between the hour and minute numbers.

We usually eat dinner at **6:30.**

▶ Use a colon before a list of things in a sentence.

I always get the same fruits at the store: apples, bananas, oranges, grapes, and pears.

▶ Use a colon after the greeting in a business letter.

Dear Store Owner: Dear Editor: Dear Mr. Clark:

SECTION

5

Grammar, Usage, and Mechanics

Hyphens and Parentheses

A **hyphen** divides a word with two or more syllables at the end of a line. The hyphen shows that the word continues on the next line.

Aunt Lynda grows plants in her green-
house.

A word can be divided with a hyphen only when at least three letters will be on each line.

Incorrect	Robert placed the pots a- bove the refrigerator.
Correct	Robert placed the pots above the refrig- erator.

Parentheses set off words that add extra information to a sentence. Parentheses are put at the beginning and end of the words.

Dogs and cats are both mammals (see page 744).

Dogs and cats are both mammals (warm-blooded vertebrates).

Try It!

A hyphen and parentheses are missing from the sentence below. Can you find where they go?

When I was little which wasn't really
that long ago I liked to eat pickle sand
wiches.

Capitalization

Beginning Words

Capitalize the first word of a sentence.

My dog always seems happy to see me.

Capitalize the first word of a quotation even if it's not the beginning of the sentence.

He laughed and said, "**T**hat joke gets funnier every time I hear it."

Names

Capitalize the names of people and pets.

Laura likes our little dog, **P**eanut.

Capitalize the pronoun *I*.

The teacher said **I** could help serve the apples.

Capitalize words used as names.

Dad and **G**randpa took us fishing at the lake.

Titles

Capitalize people's titles and initials.

Dr. Diana **A.** Taylor   **Mrs. R. J.** Sanchez

Capitalize the first word, last word, and all important words in titles of books, magazines, and newspapers.

Little House in the Big Woods is my favorite book.

Capitalize the titles of movies, plays, and TV shows.

I saw the movie *My Trip to Camp* five times.

Languages

Capitalize the names of languages.

Maria can speak both **E**nglish and **S**panish.

SECTION

5

Grammar,
Usage, and
Mechanics

Place Names and Geographic Names

Capitalize the names of countries, cities, states, oceans, rivers, mountains, and lakes.

United States of America
Boston   Oregon   Pacific Ocean
Mississippi River   Lake Erie   Rocky Mountains

Special Dates, Holidays, Historical Periods, and Special Events

Capitalize the names of months, days, and holidays.

November   Friday   Thanksgiving

Capitalize the names of historical periods and special events.

The Computer Age   The Civil War   The Olympics

Parts of Letters

Capitalize the first word in the greeting and closing of a letter.

Dear Madeline,   Yours truly,

SECTION

5

Grammar,
Usage, and
Mechanics

Abbreviations and Acronyms

Capitalize abbreviations of proper nouns.

Wed. (Wednesday)
NBA (National Basketball Association)

Capitalize acronyms.

SCUBA = Self-Contained Underwater Breathing Apparatus
HOPE = Health Opportunity for People Everywhere

Try It!

Find the three capitalization mistakes in the sentence below.
Every january, my family visits phoenix, arizona.

Writing Connection

When you're writing, be sure to capitalize the first word of every sentence. Also capitalize the first word of a quotation, proper nouns, and people's titles and initials. Capitalize the first word and all important words in the titles of books, magazines, and newspapers. The titles of movies, plays, and television shows, as well as the names of languages, need to be capitalized also. Finally, capitalize place names and geographic names; special dates, holidays, historical periods, and special events; parts of letters; and abbreviations and acronyms.

SECTION
5

Grammar, Usage, and Mechanics

Glossary

A

abbreviation the shortening of a word, such as St. for Street. Most abbreviations are followed by a period.

across-the-curriculum words words that explain terms for math, science, social studies, health, or other topics

action verbs verbs that show the actions of someone or something in a sentence

adjective a word that describes a noun or a pronoun

adverb a word that describes a verb, adjective, or another adverb. An adverb tells how, when, where, or how much something happens.

antonym a word that means the opposite, or almost the opposite, of another word

appositive a noun that follows another noun to modify or rename it

articles *a* and *an* (indefinite) and *the* (definite)

audience the person or people who read what you write

autobiography an account of a person's life written by that person

awkward sentence a confusing or unclear sentence

B

biography a written account of a person's life

body (letter) the main part of a letter. It includes the specific information you want the reader to know.

body (news story) the part of a news story that comes after the lead paragraph in which more details and information are given

body (paragraph) usually the middle part of a paragraph that gives supporting details for the topic sentence

book review a piece of writing in which you tell others what you thought about a book, either fiction or nonfiction

business letter a formal letter written to an organization or company for one special reason: to express a complaint, to express a concern, or to request information

byline tells who wrote a news story

C

caption a sentence or phrase written under a picture or illustration that tells more about the picture or explains it

chain of events a type of graphic organizer that shows events in the order in which they happen

common nouns nouns that name any person, place, thing, or idea and start with a lowercase letter

compound predicate shows two or more things about the subject

compound sentence two or more simple sentences joined together by a conjunction

compound subject two or more simple subjects connected by a conjunction

conjunction a word that connects other words or ideas. The words *and, but,* and *or* are conjunctions.

context clues word or sentence clues from the text that help you figure out the meaning of unknown words

conventions the rules one follows when writing. These include spelling, grammar, punctuation, capitalization, and usage.

D

declarative sentence a sentence that makes a statement and ends with a period

definite article the article *the* that identifies specific people, places, things, or ideas

description gives details about a person, place, thing, or action

details statements, facts, and opinions that support the main idea of a paragraph or story

dialogue the talk or conversation between two or more characters in a story or play

drafting the part of the writing process in which you write a draft, or first try, of what you want to say

E

editing/proofreading the part of the writing process where you read your writing to check for mistakes in grammar, spelling, punctuation, and capitalization

effective beginning a beginning of a story that grabs the readers' attention and makes them want to read more

effective ending an ending of a story that brings the piece of writing to a close and keeps the reader thinking about it

end rhyme using rhyming words at the end of lines of poetry

exclamatory sentence a sentence that shows strong feeling and ends with an exclamation point

F

fantasy a story that has characters, places, or events that could not exist in the real world

figurative language words or groups of words that have more than one meaning, such as similes, metaphors, and personification

folktale an old story that teaches a lesson about life. The characters in a folktale may be people or animals.

fragment an incomplete sentence. It can be missing a subject, predicate, or both.

free-verse poem poem that does not rhyme or have a pattern

future-tense verb a verb that shows what will happen later

H

helping verb the first part of a verb phrase, such as *was, were, had,* or *has*

homograph words that are spelled the same but have different meanings

homophone words that sound the same but have different spellings and meanings

I

imperative sentence a sentence that gives a command or makes a request and ends with a period or exclamation point

indefinite article the articles *a* and *an* that refer to a general group of people, places, things, or ideas

informative paragraph a paragraph that gives or explains information

informative report a report that gives information about facts, ideas, or events using nonfiction sources

informative writing a type of writing based on facts, such as giving a summary, giving directions to a location, explaining a process, or writing a report

interrogative sentence a type of sentence that asks a question and ends with a question mark

irregular plural nouns nouns that do not follow the rule for most plural nouns, such as *child* and *children*

irregular verb a verb that does not follow the rule for adding *-ed* to form the past tense

L

lead the first paragraph of a news story that answers the five Ws

learning log a type of journal or notebook in which you keep a record of what you learned about something

limerick a humorous rhyming poem where lines 1, 2, and 5 rhyme and lines 3 and 4 rhyme

linking words words that link reasons to an opinion

linking verb a state-of-being verb that links the subject of the sentence with a word in the predicate

M

main verb the last word in a verb phrase, usually an action verb

metaphor compares two unlike things without using the words *like* or *as*

mood the feeling the reader or listener gets when reading or hearing a piece of writing

mystery a piece of writing in which something happens and it is not clear how or why it happened

N

narrative paragraph a paragraph that tells a story

nonrhyming poetry poetry in which the words at the ends of the lines do not rhyme

nouns words that name everything. For example, people, places, things, and ideas are nouns.

O

observation what one sees and hears during the happening of an event

onomatopoeia a word that imitates the sound it describes, such as *swish* and *pop*

opinion the way you think or feel about something

opinion writing a type of writing in which the writer gives his or her opinion about a topic

order words words that tell in what order things happen, such as *first, next,* and *last*

P

paragraph a group of sentences about one idea

past-tense verb a verb that shows what has already happened

pattern poetry poetry in which the lines follow patterns for length and number of syllables

personal letter a letter written to a relative, a friend, or someone you would like to get to know

personal narrative a form of writing in which the writer tells something that has really happened in his or her own life

personification describes animals or things as if they were people

persuasive paragraph a paragraph that gives the writer's opinion on a topic and reasons or examples to support it

persuasive writing a type of writing in which the writer tries to persuade the reader to think, feel, or act in a certain way

plural nouns nouns that name more than one person

plural possessive nouns plural nouns that show who owns something

plural pronoun a pronoun that takes the place of a noun that names more than one person or thing

poetry a type of writing in which the sound and meaning of words are combined to create images and feelings

point of view the thoughts of the person telling the story

possessive nouns nouns that show who owns something

possessive pronoun a pronoun that shows who owns something

predicate tells what the subject is or does in a sentence

prefix a word part added to the beginning of a base word, changing the meaning

preposition a word that shows position or direction

prepositional phrase a phrase that begins with a preposition and ends with a noun or pronoun

present tense verb a verb that shows what is happening now or what happens all the time

prewriting the part of the writing process where you choose a topic, gather ideas, and make a plan

pronouns words that take the place of nouns

proofreading marks the special marks one uses when proofreading a piece of writing

proper nouns nouns that name a specific person, place, thing, or idea and always start with a capital letter

publishing the part of the writing process where you share your writing

purpose your reason for writing. The purpose could be to persuade, entertain, or inform.

R

realistic story a made-up story with characters who seem real and a plot with events that could really happen

regular verb a verb that forms the past tense by adding *-ed* to the base verb

revising a part of the writing process in which you make changes to improve what you have written

rhyming poetry poetry that uses rhyming words at the ends of the lines

rhythm a pattern of sounds in prose or poetry created by repetition of words, phrases, or sounds

S

sentence fluency the way you arrange your sentences in a piece of writing so that they read smoothly

simile compares two unlike things using the words *like* or *as*. Example: She is as cute as a button.

simple predicate the verb that tells what the subject is or does in a sentence

simple sentence has one subject and one predicate

simple subject the noun that tells who or what does or is something in a sentence

singular possessive nouns singular nouns that show who owns something

singular pronoun a pronoun that takes the place of a noun that names one person or thing

spatial order a type of graphic organizer that shows details in a chosen order, such as left-to-right or top-to-bottom

state-of-being verb a verb that does not show action but shows a condition or state of being, such as *am, become, was, feel*

story map a type of graphic organizer used to plan a story, including characters, setting, and plot

subject who or what a sentence is about

subject-verb agreement when the verb agrees with the subject of the sentence. They both must be singular or plural.

suffix a word part added to the end of a base word, changing the meaning

summary writing that tells the main idea and main points of a longer piece of writing

superlative form the form of an adjective or adverb that compares more than two people, places, or things

supporting sentence tells more about the idea in the topic sentence

surprise when something sudden or unexpected happens

suspense an excitement of not knowing what will happen. Suspense is used in adventure and mystery stories.

synonym a word that means the same, or almost the same, as another word

T

tall tale a made-up story that usually exaggerates or stretches the truth

tense the form of a verb that tells when an action happens, such as in the present, past, or future

topic sentence a sentence that tells the main idea of a paragraph. Topic sentences occur most often in expository or persuasive writing.

top-to-bottom graphic organizer a type of graphic organizer that organizes the details from a top-to-bottom approach, used when writing a description

trickster tale a story similar to a folktale in which there is a trickster character

triplet poetry that has three lines of rhyming words

U

underlining a punctuation mark used to set off the titles of books, magazines, newspapers, TV shows, movies, or plays

V

variety using different words and sentence types to make a piece of writing more interesting

Venn diagram a type of graphic organizer used to compare or contrast two things

verb phrase one or more helping verbs followed by the main verb

verbs words that show action or state-of-being

voice the tone or sound of your writing. The voice of a piece of writing changes as the audience changes.

W

web a type of graphic organizer that has the main idea inside a circle in the middle with lines connecting to bubbles that contain supporting details

writing process a plan to follow when writing. The steps are prewriting, drafting, revising, editing/proofreading, and publishing.

Index

The **index** is a list of words and page numbers. It lists the different things that are in the Handbook. The words are in alphabetical order. You look in the list for the word you want to find. Then you look at the page number of the Handbook where it can be found. The index is a good tool. Learn to use it. It can save you a lot of time.

H

have, 347
heading, 72–73, 78–79
headline, 109–111
helping verbs, 346
homograph, 326–327
homophones, 324–325
hyphens, 380

I

ideas, 234–245
    adding detail, 242–243
    combining ideas, 240–241
    taking notes, 238–239
    using dialogue, 244–245
    using drawings, 236–237
imperative sentence, 355
indefinite articles, 348
informative paragraph, 364
informative report, 114–117
informative writing, 82–123, 364
  See also,
    book review, 96–101
    directions, 105–107
    explaining a process, 102–104
    informative report, 114–117
    news story, 108–111
    research report, 118–123
    responding to literature, 88–91
    responding to nonfiction, 92–95
    summary, 84–87
    writing to inform, 112–113
initials, 376, 381
inside address, 78–79
interrogative sentence, 355
interviews, 109, 134, 152
invitation, 69
irregular plural nouns, 342
irregular verbs, 369, 371

J

journal, 64–65

K

kinds of sentences, 355

L

languages, 381
lead, 109–111
learning log, 66–67
letter of complaint, 76
letter of concern, 76
letter of request, 76
letters, 72–81, 206–207, 382
limerick, 213, 215
lines (play), 168–169, 172–173
linking verbs, 346–347
linking words, 34, 201, 204
lists, 62–63

M

main verb, 346
making a portfolio, 49
mechanics, 40, 374–383. See also,
    capitalization, 381–383
    punctuation, 374–380
metaphor, 271
mood, 287–289
mystery, 142–145

S

T

U

V

W

Photo Credits: